THE ECONOMY OF THE AMERICAN PEOPLE

Progress, Problems, Prospects

by *Gerhard Colm* and *Theodore Geiger*
with the assistance of *Manuel Helzner*

PLANNING PAMPHLET NO. 102
March 1958

NATIONAL PLANNING ASSOCIATION
Washington, D. C.

Library of Congress
Catalog Card Number
58–8790

March 1958, $2.00

CONTENTS

Background

THIS PUBLICATION serves a different purpose from that of most other staff reports of the National Planning Association. These are usually designed to provide background facts and analysis for policy statements on which our individual committee members from agriculture, business, labor, and the professions can agree. The object of this publication on *The Economy of the American People* is purely informative—to analyze the nature and prospects of the American economic system, how our private enterprise economy has been able to achieve such high productivity and living standards, why it has not succumbed to the fates predicted by the communists and other social prophets of doom, what its actual problems are and its prospects likely to be.

We in the National Planning Association have been aware of the need for such a study through our continuing relationships with teams of leaders, technicians, and students from other countries who have toured the United States under the auspices of the various governmental and privately financed programs. Many of these visitors repeatedly have urged us to set forth the nature of the American economy in readily available published form. Many of our American friends have also pointed out that, owing to NPA's representative membership, long experience, and impartial and nonpolitical character, we would be uniquely qualified to publish such a study.

These are some of the reasons which induced the NPA Board of Trustees to authorize the preparation of this report. The Board was aware of the difficulty of this undertaking and of the fact that other organizations and individuals frequently have tried to accomplish a similar purpose. At the same time, we recognized that there are many different perspectives from which the American economy could be viewed and that NPA's particular vantage point is not likely to be duplicated by others. Moreover, we were encouraged to proceed by the fact that our staff already included authors who were capable of writing the kind of report which we had in mind.

One of the authors, Gerhard Colm, is NPA's Chief Economist and also Professorial Lecturer in Economics at George Washington University in Washington, D. C. Before and since joining the NPA staff, Dr. Colm has lectured to groups of foreign visitors, introducing them to the basic facts and problems of the American economy. His experiences in Europe and Asia and in the United States have made him especially aware of the questions to which foreign observers of the American economy seek answers.

The other author, Theodore Geiger, NPA's Chief of International Studies, has been trained as an economic and social historian, and has professional experience as an economist, especially in the international field. Dr. Geiger provided particularly the historical and sociological dimensions of the study, and took primary responsibility for treating the international aspects of the American economy.

The authors were ably assisted by Manuel Helzner, associate economist at NPA, who, in addition to providing statistical data, contributed to the study in numerous ways.

This report was reviewed, discussed, and approved for publication by the NPA Steering Committee. We are grateful to Mrs. Virginia D. Parker for making the manuscript more readable. Thanks are also due to a number of friends here and abroad who have read and criticized the report in draft.

H. CHRISTIAN SONNE
Chairman, NPA Board of Trustees

THE ECONOMY OF THE AMERICAN PEOPLE

Progress, Problems, Prospects

Introduction

NO ONE can fail to notice the drastic changes which have been taking place in technology during recent decades. Jet planes in the sky, television sets in the living room, electrical and electronic equipment in the kitchen, automatic controls in the factory, nuclear reactors in the power plant—all of these and more are here for everyone to see.

There is less awareness that the way in which our economic system works also has been changing drastically. Out of nineteenth-century capitalism, a new American economy has been evolving. This economy is about as similar to the capitalism of old as a jet airplane is to the Wright brothers' original model. And yet much of the discussion of our present economic system is conducted as though no change had taken place. Perhaps this is because most Americans have been too busy living and working amid these changes to think much about their significance or their important effect on the development of civilization.

The purpose of this report is to describe the leading characteristics of our new economy. We attempt to depict the American economy in action—how it works, what its major achievements and shortcomings are, what problems it still must solve, and what its prospects are for the future. In emphasizing both accomplishments and shortcomings, we are committing what some social scientists may regard as a mortal intellectual sin. For, by so doing, we are confessing that we have approached the subject with some idea of desirable objectives. Such an idea, nonetheless, is indispensable, for only in the light of objectives does it make sense to speak of achievements and to discuss unsolved problems. We begin, therefore, by stating our criteria for judging the achievements and shortcomings of the American economy.

Certain objectives have always been common to all economic systems, whatever their cultures. People everywhere and at all times need food, shelter, and clothing, and desire the various amenities of life. All societies—all organized groups of human beings living and working together—need means for maintaining internal order and external security. Also, societies need to conserve and expand natural resources and the means of production for future generations.

These manifold objectives can be achieved best through the economical use of resources, that is, through producing the largest possible amount of goods and services with the available means—manpower, materials, and knowledge. Thus, the amount actually produced during a given period compared with the total possible production is one of the main yardsticks for measuring economic achievement. This criterion can be applied to all societies irrespective of their particular aspirations and institutional structures.

The largest possible production and consumption is not, however, the sole objective of an economic system. An economy is itself only a means to the achievement of other, more fundamental, social and individual values. The specific values served by an economic system depend upon the historical culture of which the economy is an intrinsic part. Within each society, there usually is a broad common ground concerning general objectives, but there are differences as to specific goals to be sought by economic means, differences which reflect the divergent interests or traditions of particular groups making up the society.

For Americans, conflicting views about the objectives of the economic system became a major issue of national policy in the early years of the Republic. To Thomas Jefferson, the ultimate values of society were "Life, Liberty and the pursuit of Happiness." These, he believed, could best be ensured by an economy of independent family farms and small workshops. His opponent, Alexander Hamilton, had a vision of American national greatness made possible by the power and wealth of a growing population and an expanding industrial system. In the past century and a half, Americans have been fortunate in achieving national power and wealth beyond even Hamilton's imagination without sacrificing the Jeffersonian values of individual independence and responsibility.

However passionately the realization of these ideals was sought, their embodiment in social institutions has not been rigid and doctrinaire, but flexible and practical. Throughout the nation's history, there have been recurring waves of reform. But in all of these, there has been a working compromise between Jeffersonian and Hamiltonian objectives, which reflected the possibilities and limitations of the times. An agrarian economy of small farms was the relevant embodiment of the Jeffersonian ideal of individual independence in the late eighteenth and early nineteenth centuries. But in the mid-twentieth century, only an ineffectual nostalgia would seek individual independence through reversion to a predominantly agrarian society.

Today, the continuing task of achieving Jeffersonian independence and self-responsibility along with Hamiltonian wealth and power involves different social possibilities and limitations. It has become necessary to reconcile the concentrations of economic and political power required for economic growth and national security with the predominance of private, decentralized decision making and action needed to preserve freedom and individuality.

Americans are not likely to be any more disposed in the future than they are now to accept as a goal a continuous rise in total production if it means a society of human robots. Nor would it make much difference whether such robotized men and women were commanded by an all-powerful state, as in communistic societies, or by all-powerful captains of industry, as might have been the case had nineteenth-century laissez-faire capitalism survived. In the last analysis, the fundamental issue facing the present generation of Americans is not agrarianism versus industrialism or socialism versus capitalism. The question is: Can the American society succeed in combining the benefits of large-scale organization in the economy and in government with the greatest possible freedom of individual choice and the fullest possible realization of the potentialities of the individual? In taking a fresh look at the trends and prospects of the American economy, we are searching for an answer to this crucial question.

The all too frequent discussion of the American economy from the point of view of socialism versus capitalism has seriously distorted the question. In such discussions, there are extremists on both sides. On the one hand, there are—abroad as well as at home—panegyrists of the American economic system who regard it as the embodiment of the pure laissez-faire ideal. To them, the greatest good for the greatest number is automatically guaranteed when private individuals and organizations are completely free to pursue their own self-interests. In their view, injustices and inadequacies result from the interference of a meddlesome government with the free workings of the system, and all problems would disappear if the government would leave everything alone.

On the other hand, there is the Marxist view, which is even less valid, either as description of, or prescription for, the American economy. Marxist theory has insisted in the face of all evidence that American "capitalism" must be characterized by the deepening misery of the "masses" as wealth is increasingly concentrated in the hands of the "monopolists." It adheres to the doctrine that the inevitable collapse which must follow from this process is only being postponed by America's "imperialistic" drive for foreign markets, overseas investments, and wars. This fantastic picture of the nature and problems of the American economy could be disregarded as pure propaganda were it not that it is seriously believed, at least in part, by many noncommunist intellectuals in other countries of the Free World.

The distortions of the laissez-faire idolators and the fantasies of the Marxist detractors do equal violence to the facts of the American economy. We believe that the perspective in which we have chosen to view our economy is less susceptible to such errors because it is indigenous to the American system and to its social tradition. It is difficult to avoid exaggerations and blindspots of one's own, and we freely admit that one of our purposes is to show what we believe makes life worth living under American economic and social conditions. Yet, while we take pride in the promise of the American economy, we recognize its deficiencies and remaining problems. An understanding of what has been accomplished is necessary for insight into the nature of the problems still confronting Americans and of the means for tackling them. Perhaps what we like best about our system is that—as in all democracies—every citizen has a responsibility to recognize the economy's shortcomings and to work for its improvement. Only through this process can the American economy move toward the fulfillment of its potentialities.

Part One

How the American Economy Achieves High Productivity and Consumption

It would be pleasant to be able to present an uncomplicated, uncluttered explanation of the way America has achieved its unprecedented productivity and high standard of living. But the American economy is as complex as an intricate piece of machinery. Its output depends not only on many different parts, but on maintaining a delicate balance one with the other. In a sense, it is somewhat surprising that this mechanism has not flown apart under the stresses and strains created in a democracy by the opposing pressures exerted from the widely differing geographic regions and the multiplicity of special interest groups in the United States. And yet, there can be no question that the machine not only has continued to work, but that, over time, its make-up has been substantially changed and its efficiency improved and increased. In the following chapters, we attempt to show how this has come about.

The first chapter presents a variety of facts and figures on production, income, and consumption in the United States and other countries. The statistics given in that condensed survey may not be new or necessary to many readers. Yet, taken together, they offer a starting point for an understanding of the interrelated factors entering into American productivity.

Chapters II through VIII seek answers to two questions: What are the main factors that have brought about the rise in American productivity and made possible so large an increase in the American standard of living? What is the likelihood of a continuation of these trends for the future? The discussion centers on the contributions to productivity of such factors as natural resources, labor, management, research and technology, capital, government, and, finally, the institutions, motives, and values which have conditioned these elements in the American economy.

The purpose of Part One is to describe—not to commend or criticize—how each of these particular factors contributes to productivity. We might point out here, however, that in no case have we found perfection; in each, there are areas which should be and can be improved. A hint of such deficiencies appears in the description of each factor. However, our analysis of such problems and the ways in which they are being tackled by public and private policies is reserved for Part Two.

Chapter I

Some Facts and Figures

JUST HOW HIGH are production and consumption in the United States? And how do they compare with economic achievements in other countries?

- ***Total production in the United States is more than double that in the boom year 1929 and can be expected to continue to increase for the next decade at approximately the same rate of growth.***
- ***Production, income, and consumption per capita are high compared to previous decades; they are also much higher than in any other country.***
- ***The United States comprises only 6 percent of the world's population, yet accounts for more than a third of the total industrial production of the planet.***
- ***The benefits of large-scale production are more widely shared among Americans than ever before or in most other countries.***
- ***The country is better prepared to counteract economic instability than at any time in the past.***

These are bare statements. Supported by other figures, however, they can convey some idea of the quantitative dimensions of the American economy and of its characteristic differences from other economies.

A few words of warning on the interpretation of these figures and those to follow are in order. The per capita figures given for such measurements as income and earnings, food supplies, housing, and other aspects of living standards in the United States relate to the "average" American. While some Americans are better off than these figures indicate, there are still remnants of poverty which are lost in these averages. Also, international comparisons of production and consumption are hazardous. They, too, fail to show the gradations necessary to obtain a true picture of both advances and delays in standards of living, either in the United States or in other countries. Nevertheless, international statistical comparisons can help in providing perspective on some of the features of the American economy which need to be examined.

There is another serious drawback in relying too heavily on statistical measures; they unavoidably fail to reflect accurately the important and far-reaching intangible characteristics which exist in all countries. Monetary and physical comparisons alone do not adequately express either the noneconomic values created by productive processes or the qualitative aspects of different kinds and levels of consumption. Production and consumption of goods and services, valued at market prices, cannot measure the full social significance of economic activity. The work of a scientist, for example, may command very little payment while it is under way, even though his inventions or discoveries may turn out to be of great future significance. Many of the most important medical discoveries have brought very little financial return to those who made them. Dedicated teachers, notoriously underpaid in comparison to the importance of their role, inspire the curiosity, imagination, and daring which lead to progress and change. Similarly, the activities of an artist who does not immediately sell his paintings will, in strictly monetary terms, be valued at zero even though he may be contributing incalculable value to the cultural life of the nation.

Despite these inadequacies of statistical description, a few of the more significant quantitative comparisons may help to round out understanding of the factors responsible for the achievements of the American economy as well as for the deficiencies which still remain.

Recent Developments in the United States

Over the past generation, the economy of the American people has experienced some major contrasts—the boom of the 1920's, the severe depression of the 1930's, the war economy and the postwar adjustment of the 1940's, and the expansion of the 1950's. Yet, despite the inhibiting effect of the depression and the diversion of resources into military production, productive capacity for peaceful uses has increased enormously since 1929. At the end of 1957, total production, measured in constant dollars, was more than double that of the boom year 1929, and more than 40 percent above a decade ago. Since 1929, there also has been a rise in per capita personal consumption of more than 50 percent.

Productivity—the output of goods and services per man-hour—is the key to this high and rising standard of living. It is productivity which has made possible the ability to produce greater and greater quantities of goods and services out of currently available resources. It is productivity which has sustained a high level of consumption, even while the average work week has declined. And it is productivity which largely accounts for the economic growth and the relatively high degree of economic stability in recent years.

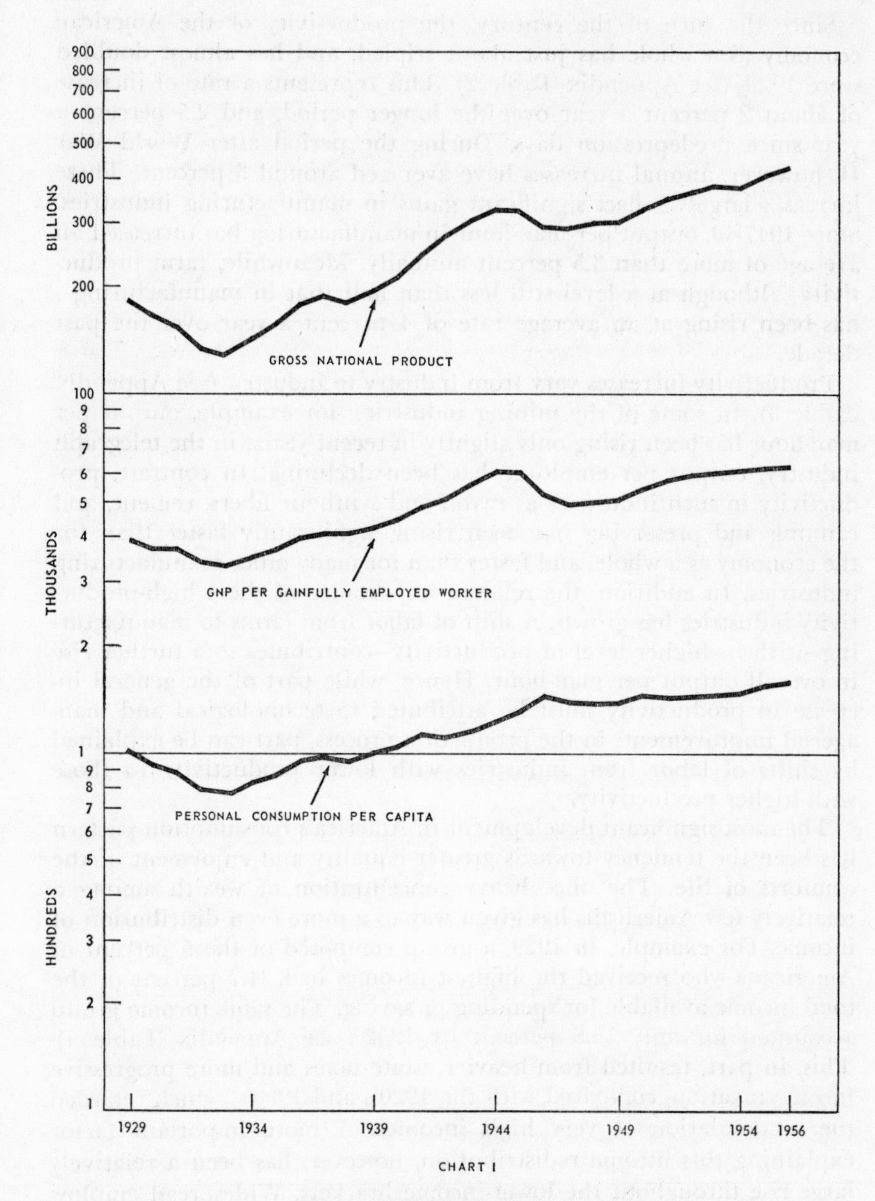

CHART I

ECONOMIC GROWTH INDICATORS, 1929 - 1956
(in 1956 dollars)

Source: See Appendix Table 1.

Since the turn of the century, the productivity of the American economy as a whole has just about tripled, and has almost doubled since 1929 (see Appendix Table 2). This represents a rate of increase of about 2 percent a year over the longer period, and 2.5 percent a year since predepression days. During the period after World War II, however, annual increases have averaged around 3 percent. These increases largely reflect significant gains in manufacturing industries. Since 1947-49, output per man-hour in manufacturing has increased an average of more than 3.5 percent annually. Meanwhile, farm productivity—although at a level still less than half that in manufacturing—has been rising at an average rate of 4 percent a year over the past decade.

Productivity increases vary from industry to industry (see Appendix Table 3). In some of the mining industries, for example, output per man-hour has been rising only slightly in recent years; in the telegraph industry, output per employee has been declining. In contrast, productivity in such industries as rayon and synthetic fibers, cement, and canning and preserving has been rising significantly faster than for the economy as a whole, and faster than for many other manufacturing industries. In addition, the relative importance of these high-productivity industries has grown. A shift of labor from farms to manufacturing—with its higher level of productivity—contributes to a further rise in overall output per man-hour. Hence, while part of the general increase in productivity must be attributed to technological and managerial improvements in the production process, part can be explained by shifts of labor from industries with lower productivity to those with higher productivity.

The most significant development in America's consumption pattern has been the tendency towards greater equality and enjoyment of the comforts of life. The once heavy concentration of wealth among a relatively few Americans has given way to a more even distribution of income. For example, in 1929, a group composed of the 5 percent of Americans who received the highest incomes had 34.7 percent of the total income available for spending or saving. The same income group accounted for only 15.8 percent by 1952 (see Appendix Table 4). This, in part, resulted from heavier estate taxes and more progressive income taxation, compared with the 1920's and 1930's, which retarded the accumulation of very high incomes. A more important factor explaining this income redistribution, however, has been a relatively large rise throughout the lower-income brackets. Widespread employment opportunities, plus increasingly effective collective bargaining and the establishment of minimum-wage standards, have lifted the income levels of the lower-wage groups closer to those of the higher-income groups.

Two or three decades ago, the head of a low-income family—if he were employed—usually worked long hours for an inadequate wage. Only if several members also worked full or part time could the family

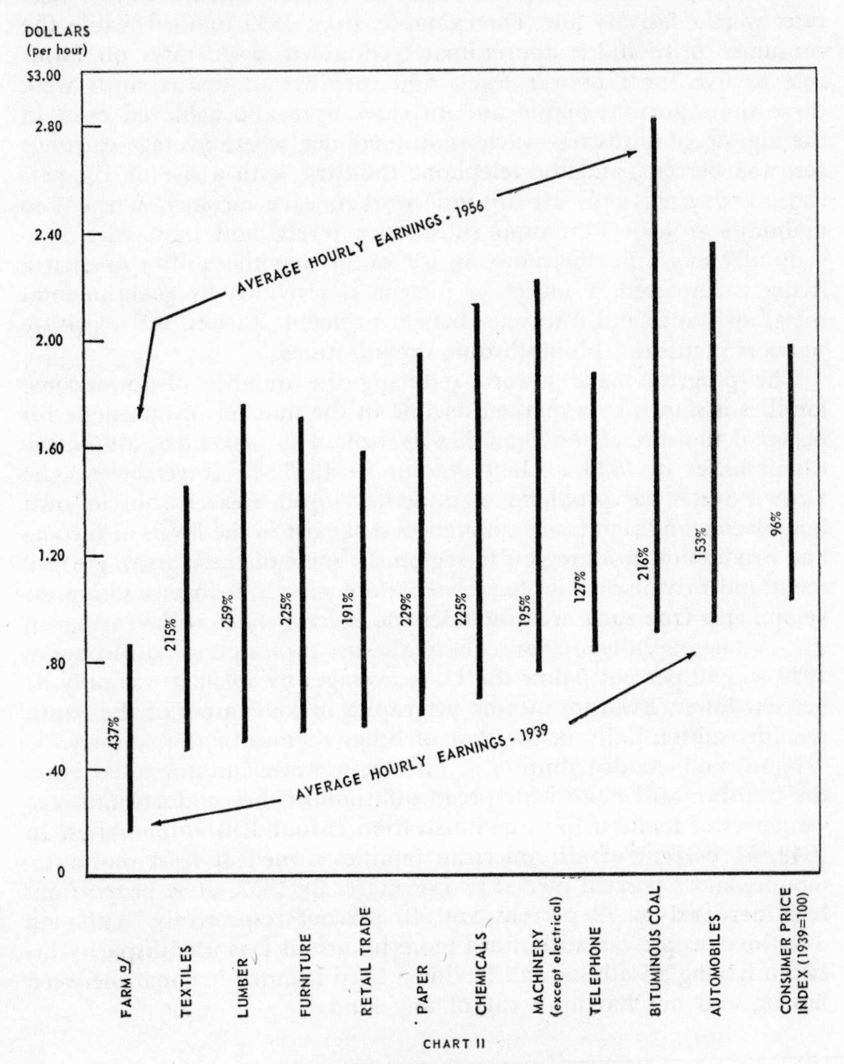

CHART II

INCREASE IN AVERAGE HOURLY EARNINGS FOR SELECTED INDUSTRIES 1939 - 56 (percent increase over 1939)

a/ Average hourly wage rate without board or room. For 1939 - average daily wage rate divided by average hours per day.

Note: Consumer price index (1947=100) rose 96% between 1939-56.

Source: See Appendix Table 5.

obtain a minimum subsistence income. The problem then was the inadequacy of basic wage rates in many full-time occupations. Since the 1930's, however, average hourly earnings for the American worker have risen substantially—particularly in those industries where wage rates were relatively low. For example, from 1939 to 1956, while the consumer price index approximately doubled, wage rates on farms rose to five times prewar levels and earnings in textile mills were three times greater. Significant increases were also achieved even in the high-wage industries—such as automobiles, where average earnings rose 153 percent, and the telephone industry, with a rise of 127 percent. Today, virtually all full-time workers earn incomes sufficient to maintain at least minimum subsistence levels, and most earn substantially more. Furthermore, in the event that the ability to earn a living is impaired, a source of income is provided by governmental social assistance and insurance benefit payments, as well as by private pension plans and philanthropic organizations.

The progress made toward reducing the number of low-income families is shown by a marked decline in the number of families with personal incomes of less than $2,000—from 41.5 percent of all American families in 1929 to 18.9 percent in 1953-54.[1] Nevertheless, the United States has problems of underdeveloped areas within its own boundaries, and significant differences still exist in the levels of income and production from region to region. In some of these areas, government and private policies have been quite successful in promoting development. One such area includes the several states which make up the Tennessee Valley region. There, the per capita personal income in 1929 was 49 percent below the U. S. average; by 1956, it was only 31 percent lower. Even so, income per capita in some areas of the South remains substantially below that of other regions of the country.

Figures on the distribution of income, however, do not fully reveal the trend toward more widespread diffusion of the comforts and conveniences of modern life. An illustration is found in automobiles. In 1949, 51 percent of all American families owned at least one automobile, and 3 percent owned two or more. By 1957, these proportions had increased to 72 percent and 10 percent respectively. Although wealthier people can still afford more luxurious cars, the disparity between having a Cadillac and having a Ford is much less than between having and not having a car of any kind.

---

[1]Families include unattached individuals. In order to make the figures comparable, the limit of $2,000 is expressed in constant purchasing power of the 1950 price level. See, Selma Goldsmith, "Relation of Census Income Distribution Statistics to Other Income Data," unpublished paper presented to Conference on Research in Income and Wealth, March 23-24, 1956, Table 8.

A further demonstration of better living is found in the field of housing, where government programs have made it possible for millions of families to purchase better homes than they otherwise could have afforded. Home ownership is becoming the typical mode of life for the average American family, although some still live in overcrowded apartments or run-down tenements. In 1940, 43.6 percent of nonfarm American families lived in homes they owned themselves. By 1956, this percentage had advanced to 60 percent. Furthermore, 80 percent of all American families had a television set and one or more radios.

Other values also enter into the growth in better living standards. Government activities—federal, state, and local—now provide many essential services to the people, including education, social welfare, public health, and parks and other recreational facilities. Formerly, mainly wealthy people could afford a higher education for their children. Although the United States is still far from a situation in which higher education depends exclusively on the ability of the student, nevertheless, a remarkable extension of college education has been achieved. In 1957, of the young Americans aged eighteen to twenty-four, roughly 15 percent was enrolled in colleges or universities as contrasted with less than 3 percent in 1900. Or another example. A generation ago, relatively few Americans could afford, or had the time for, a vacation and travel. Today, most Americans have paid vacations, and travel for recreation and pleasure in such vast numbers that satisfaction of their needs has created a major service industry. Medical and hospital services, too, are being brought within reach of a growing number of Americans, regardless of whether or not they can pay for such care.

Thus, in the United States, a combination of factors has helped to increase and more equally distribute the comforts of life, particularly in the interest of people with lower incomes. These factors are: a real reduction in the inequality of income distribution, a general rise in income and consumption levels, and the addition of government programs and public services.

Since the end of World War II, the American economy has—with only minor interruptions—maintained steady growth. Only for a few months during the past decade did unemployment exceed 5 percent of the civilian labor force; on the average, it amounted to less than 4 percent. Some of this unemployment was caused by seasonal factors, temporary layoffs, or changes from one job to another—which are not unexpected in a full employment economy.

On the whole, the nature of the relatively low unemployment during the past decade is different from that of earlier periods; it no longer means complete destitution. In 1957, for example, almost half of the unemployed were without work for four weeks or less. In general, most unemployed workers know that they have a good chance of finding other employment within a short time. There has been little of the frustration of the depression periods of the past. However, in some depressed areas and in some industries, there was protracted unemployment. This type of longer-lasting unemployment, as well as a relative scarcity of jobs for aged workers and the widowed, have created serious problems. Both private groups and public agencies have been set up to help alleviate this situation through worker placement and community rehabilitation programs. Many workers are able to accumulate a small savings reserve to tide them over a short period of unemployment. In addition, more than half of the unemployed collect government unemployment insurance benefits to help sustain their living standards. And some labor unions provide supplemental income payments to unemployed members.

Based on past experience, some observers have maintained that rapid economic expansion would be accompanied by either considerable economic instability or rising prices. In the postwar years—those immediately following World War II and after the Korean outbreak—prices did increase sharply. Indeed, in recent years, the price level has been rising in the United States, as in most other countries of the world. While the rise from the spring of 1951 to the end of 1957

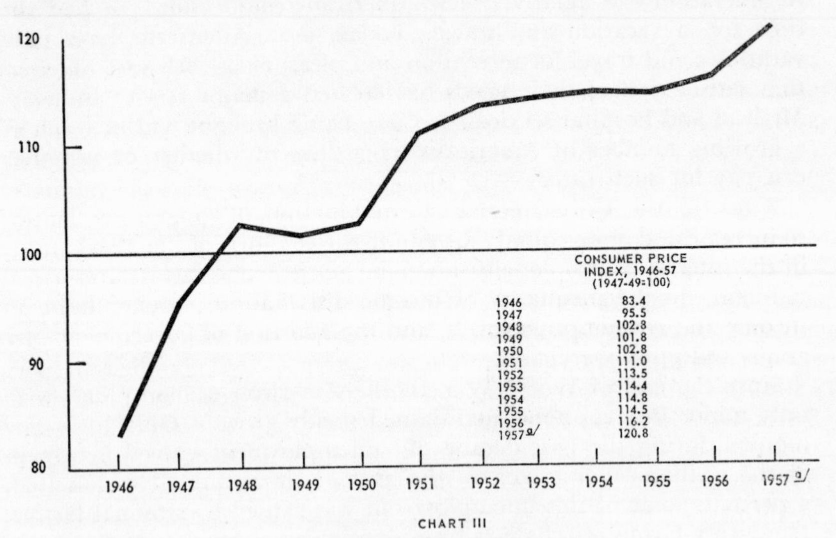

CHART III

CONSUMER PRICE INDEX, 1946-57 (1947-49=100)

a/ July, 1957.

Sources: Historical Supplement to Economic Indicators - 1957, p. 53.
Economic Indicators, September 1957.

has not been alarming—less than 10 percent over the entire period—it demonstrates that the problem of price stabilization in a full employment economy still has not been finally solved.

The United States has enjoyed a long, hardly interrupted, period of high and rising employment, production, and consumption. But this fact in itself should not lead to the conclusion that serious economic fluctuations need no longer be feared. Such complacency would be as unjustified as to have inferred from the depression years of the 1930's that the American economy had entered a period of continuing stagnation which would last indefinitely. Businessmen, workers, the government, and Americans in general are much better equipped to adopt prompt and effective countermeasures in the event a serious economic slump should occur. And there is a widespread determination that these anti-depression tools should be used promptly when needed.

International Comparisons

Statistical comparisons of standards of living show that Americans not only consume more goods and services per capita than other peoples, but they share more equally in the benefits of large-scale production than most. Nevertheless, in some measurements of particular aspects of living standards, one or more industrial countries still rank higher than the United States. And figures which are much higher for the United States than for some of the less developed countries—if accepted without some consideration of each country's state of development—tend to belittle the actual economic achievements of others. A realistic appraisal must take into account the problems, difficulties, and obstacles which the less developed countries must face and overcome in their efforts to achieve even a modest advance in per capita production and consumption.

Nevertheless, expressed in monetary terms, both production per gainfully employed person and consumption per capita in the United States are about two to three times greater than in many European countries and about eight to ten times greater than in most other countries. Similar disparities appear if the comparisons are measured in physical terms. Estimates of diet content, for example, show that nearly 60 percent of the world's population lives in areas where the supply of food is not sufficient to provide for each inhabitant 2,200 calories a day, which under most environmental conditions is at—or probably below—minimum nutritional requirements.

In the United States and in the more industrialized countries of the world, nutritional needs generally are more than satisfied, but caloric levels in most of the less developed countries are often below what is necessary or desirable. This is not to say that malnutrition and dietary deficiencies are nonexistent in the United States. However, the over-all level of nutritional adequacy in America is significantly higher than in most other areas of the world.

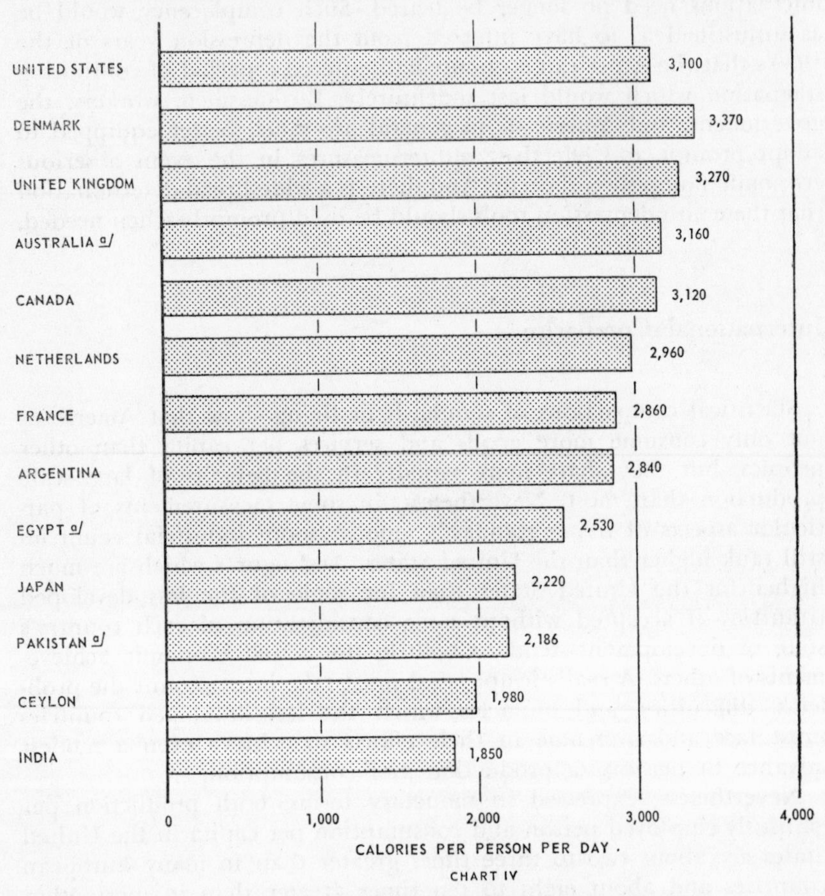

CHART IV

CALORIC CONTENT OF FOOD SUPPLIES, 1954 - 55
(calories per person per day)

a/ 1953 - 54.

Source: United Nations Statistical Yearbook, 1956.

Another comparison of physical standards is reflected in housing conditions in various countries. There are in the United States anywhere from 10 to 50 percent more dwelling units per person than in parts of Europe or Latin America. In many other countries, there would be an even starker contrast in terms of the quantity of available housing; not to mention the qualitative differences in sanitary facilities, light, water, and recreational space. But again, the figures could be deceptive if they were interpreted to mean that the United States is free of crowding and slums.

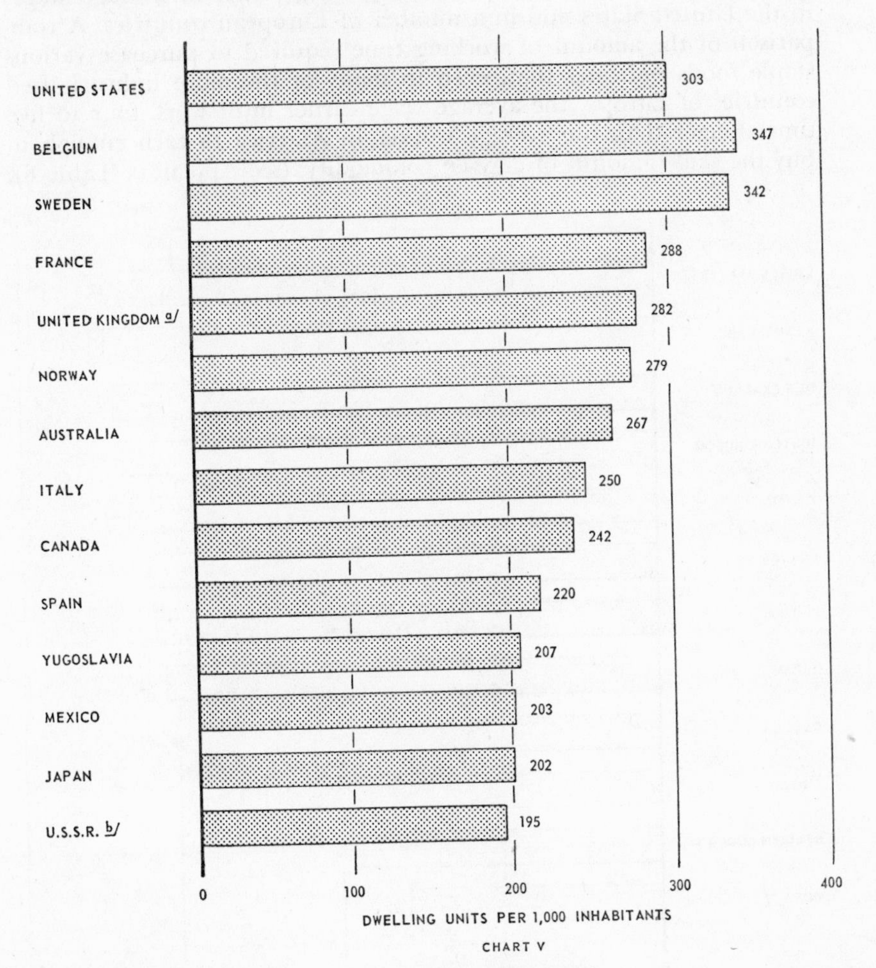

CHART V

AVAILABLE HOUSING

a/ Excludes vacant dwelling units.

b/ Urban districts only.

Note: Data refer to years 1953 or 1954 except for United States, Spain, and Mexico - 1950; Japan - 1955; Canada - 1956.

Sources: U. S. Census of Housing - 1950.
The European Housing Situation, United Nations, January 1956.
Division of Housing and Planning, Pan America Union, 1956.

Figures on income levels do not by themselves indicate the full extent of the disparity between wages in the United States and those abroad. Price levels for similar items vary widely among different countries, as do consumption patterns. Despite this, some attempts have been made to estimate the purchasing power of average wages in the United States and in a number of European countries. A comparison of the amount of working time required to purchase various staple foods indicates that, even in many of the more industrialized countries of Europe, the average wage earner must work four to five times longer than the average worker in America to earn enough to buy the same amount of a given commodity (see Appendix Table 6).

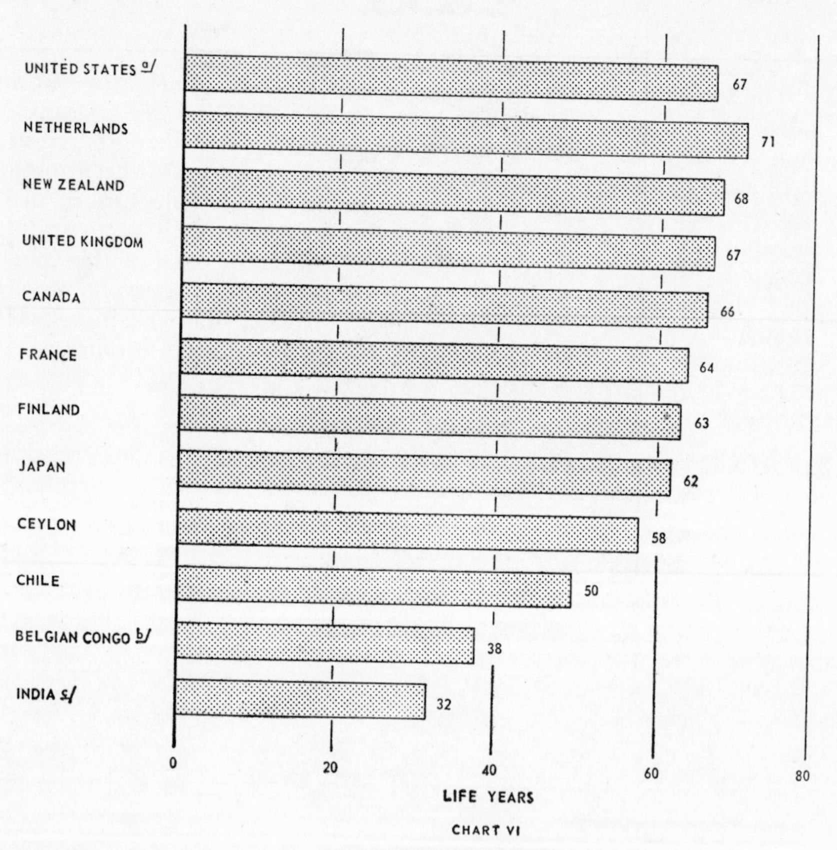

CHART VI

LIFE EXPECTANCY OF MALES AT BIRTH (1950 - 52)

a/ White males.

b/ Africans.

c/ 1941-50.

Source: United Nations Statistical Yearbook, 1956.

Differences in living standards become even more meaningful when considered in terms of average life expectancy. While advances in medical science and public hygiene have contributed to longer life everywhere, there are still variations from country to country. The living span for many people in some of the less developed areas of the world is significantly shorter than in some of the more industrialized countries. This disparity can be attributed in large measure to the comforts of life, if "comforts" are defined not merely as automobiles and telephones, but also as doctors, medical care, public hygiene, and leisure time.

The foregoing figures, rough and condensed as they are, bear out a fairly general recognition that American productivity and consumption are high and that they have moved steadily upward in recent decades. The interrelated elements that have entered into this growth are less well-known. Some have received too much emphasis in discussions of the American economy; others have had too little attention. In the following evaluation of the more important parts of this complex economic machinery, we shall examine what each does, how well they fit together, and whether certain adjustments are needed in some to maintain a desirable rate of growth in the American economy.

Chapter II

Natural Resources

IT IS OFTEN SAID that a country which enjoys a high standard of living must be particularly blessed by nature. Is this the case with the United States? Are the American climate so favorable, the soil so fertile, the mineral resources so rich, that the United States inevitably would have become a populous and productive nation?

Within the far-flung boundaries of the United States, virtually all types of the temperate zone's weather can be found—hot, cold, wet, dry, and in between. On the whole, the American climate is not so conducive to long and intensive hours of work as are, for example, the milder winters and cooler summers of Western Europe. Unquestionably, however, it is more favorable to intensive physical effort than is the climate of many tropical countries. Aside from this general influence, climate has been chiefly important in American agriculture.

Agricultural Resources

There can be no question of the present high productivity of American agriculture; but whether this is primarily the result of unusually fertile soil and favorable climate is open to serious doubt.

In the earlier periods of development, American agriculture had the advantages of open frontiers and empty spaces, with rich soils never before tilled, where grasses and forests held the moisture and prevented erosion. There was less incentive than in densely populated parts of the world to husband the fertility of the soil. When natural fertility declined in one clearing, farmers could move on and open another, and not much expense was involved in pulling up stakes and resettling. With only a few simple tools, some seeds, and a willingness to work long and hard, the farmer and his family could set up a new home and begin operations on virgin soil. However, even with that good, deep soil, the farmer could not produce much more food and fiber than he and his family needed for themselves. In 1820, for example, one farm worker in the United States produced only enough for about four people.

That situation has long since changed. Today, one American farm worker produces enough food and fiber to take care of the needs of twenty-six persons. The prices of good farm land are high and have been rising, and the need and desire for larger farms are growing. An American who expects to succeed at farming—no matter how hard-working he may be—must not only make substantial investments for farm land, but also in farm machinery, improved breeds of seeds and animals, fertilizers, insecticides, soil conservation and irrigation, plus technical and managerial training in their use. Much of his success in achieving greater production is tied to the work of other people—work on products and implements produced in the chemical, machinery, electrical, automotive, and other industries; on discoveries in private and public research laboratories; on the buyers and distributors of farm products; and on those who keep him regularly informed on new methods and techniques.

During the last two decades especially, notable advances in agricultural productivity have coincided with the large increases in investment and rapid technological improvements on farms. Output per acre of most crops in the United States is considerably higher now than in the early 1940's. More significant than increased acreage yields, however, is the yield of the individual farm worker. Agricultural output per man-hour has more than doubled in the United States since 1929. Americans are contributing about 20 percent of the world's agricultural production with less than 2 percent of the world's agricultural labor. Judged by any standard—output per man or per acre, quality of products, size of farms, size of investments, the standards of farm living, or others—the changes in American agriculture have been spectacular in recent years.

While these far-reaching changes have been taking place, one basic characteristic of American agriculture has remained unchanged. Family farms—traditional in the United States—are still predominant in American agriculture. This is a tremendous advantage since the family farm offers greater incentive for individual effort and care than any other farm system. Similarly, a deep interest in technological innovation is by no means new. During the last hundred years, the federal and state governments have undertaken a variety of programs to promote agricultural research, education, and efficiency. Succeeding generations of farmers and their families have had access to more and more educational opportunities and farm services—to vocational agricultural high schools; agricultural colleges and experiment stations; face-to-face counseling from government specialists and from businessmen who buy farm products or sell the varied supplies farmers need; participation in farm organizations; and a wealth of free or near-free pamphlets, journals, and bulletins on all phases of agricultural development. All of these have stimulated growth in the productivity, profitability, and satisfactions of family farming.

Certainly, production on every farm is still affected—in some years and some areas, drastically so—by weather, soil, and topography. However, these natural phenomena by no means have the influence on productivity of three other factors, which relate only indirectly to climate and original soil fertility. These are: the family-type farm; the relatively large size of family farms; and the high degree of technological innovation and capital investment on family farms.

A surprising number of Americans have unrealistic ideas of present-day farming and farmers. They range all the way from those who think of all farming as a simple operation, easily entered with no special training and very little investment, to those who believe family farming is being replaced by enormous corporate farms which are now responsible for the ever-increasing plentitude of foods and fibers. Nothing could be farther from the truth than either of these extremes, but there is some excuse for a lack of understanding. There are wide differences among the 4.7 million American farms reported in the 1954 Census of Agriculture.[1] They range in size, anywhere from one to 100,000 acres; in annual sales, from $200 to $1 million; in the kind of crops and animals grown and the extent of diversification on each farm; in the degree of mechanization and the use of hired labor; and they have many other variations.

The 1954 Census figures give us an idea of the average American farm, while pointing up the many differences by breakdowns into rough economic classifications. First is a division between "commercial" and "noncommercial" farms. The commercial group includes all full-time farms, divided into six "economic classes," with sales ranging from $250 a year to $25,000 or more. Noncommercial farms are those operated on a part-time or residential basis, where 100 days or more a year are worked off the farm or where off-farm income is bigger than farm income, and sales of farm products do not exceed $1,200 a year.

In 1954, more than 80 percent of all full-time commercial farms had annual sales ranging from $1,200 to $25,000 a year; they accounted for 70 percent of all commercial farmland and 67 percent of the total value of farm products sold. In contrast, only 4 percent of all the commercial farms had annual sales of $25,000 or more, but these large-scale farms operated on 25 percent of all farmland and sold 32 percent of all farm products.

An attempt to picture the average American commercial farm would show a farm family with an operation something like this.

---

[1]The nature of today's farms and differences among them are illuminated in *Popular Report—The American Farmer in 1954,* seventh of the Special Reports which make up Vol. III of the *United States Census of Agriculture: 1954,* U. S. Department of Commerce, Bureau of the Census, Washington, 1956.

The farmer would have about 310 acres, of which more than 40 percent would be in cropland. He would have an investment of about $25,000 in land and buildings, $4,000 in machinery, and $3,200 in livestock. He would spend something like $1,000 to hire machines or labor or a combination of both; and the sale of his products would amount to about $7,400.

On this average farm, electricity (used on more than 90 percent of American farms), and running water not only would make for more efficient farm operations, but for more household efficiency and a healthier and better-fed family, with more leisure time. Telephones and radios would supplement information provided in magazines and daily papers. And, if a broadcasting station were nearby, a television set would be likely. In 1950, less than 3 percent of farmers had television sets, but by 1957, more than 60 percent owned them. With improvements in communication and transportation, the farmer could react more rapidly to market developments. And the greater mobility of the farm family would permit members to take advantage of more educational, cultural, and social opportunities.

Even more difficult than describing the average American farm is comparing it with the typical European or Asian farm. In other parts of the world, the family farmer cultivates a relatively small plot of arable land. In Belgium, for example, roughly three-quarters of all farms have less than 2.5 acres (1 hectare) of land. The small size of such farms limits the efficiency of operation and the use of machinery. However, the fact that these few acres undergo intensive cultivation is one reason why average yields per acre for some crops in America are still lower than those in some other parts of the world. Comparison of the average size of farms, therefore, may not reflect the differences in the characteristics of the family farm in the United States and those in most countries.

Some farms are so large that they require hired labor, which in many types of farm production has proved less efficient than family operation. However, most large farms in the United States can be operated by family members with a minimum of hired labor because of advanced farming methods and equipment. The extent to which the American family farm has become more of a technical operation than a manual activity is indicated by the extensive use of labor-saving equipment. In 1954, for example, 72 percent of commercial farms were using tractors and 53 percent had motor trucks. This shift to mechanization is further illustrated by the fact that there were less than 5 million horses and mules on farms in 1954 compared with about 25 million head in 1920. Between 1950 and 1954, the commercial farms added 37 percent more grain combines, about 50 percent more corn pickers, and made similar sizable additions of milking machines, balers, harvesters, and so on. This increased mechanization on family farms

Table I

Size and Distribution of Agriculture Holdings—1950

Country	Average size of agr. holding (hectares)	Percent of holdings under one hectare	Percent of holdings under 10 hectares
United States	215.6	1[1]	25[4]
Belgium	1.9	75	95
Canada	113.1	[2]	17[5]
Costa Rica	42.1	na	54
Denmark	17.5	1	46
El Salvador	8.8	40	89
Finland	33.3	44[3]	84
Western Germany	10.9	14	76
Honduras	16.1	10	75
Netherlands	5.7	41	82
Norway	20.2	46	94
Philippines	3.5	19	94
Uruguay	199.7	na	26

na Not available.
[1] Percent of holdings under 1.2 hectares.
[2] Less than .5 percent.
[3] Percent of holdings under 2 hectares.
[4] Percent of holdings under 11.7 hectares.
[5] Percent of holdings under 28.3 hectares.
NOTE: One hectare equals 2.47 acres

SOURCES: *Report on the 1950 World Census of Agriculture*, Vol. I, Food and Agriculture Organization, Rome, Italy, 1955; *United States Census of Agriculture*, U. S. Department of Commerce, Washington, D.C., 1956.

has greatly reduced the requirement for agricultural workers, and has made more manpower available for manufacturing and service trades.

In the past twenty-five years, while productivity was increasing, the total number of American farms has steadily decreased, but the total acreage in farms has not. Much of the land which has become available as farmers moved to other jobs or quit farming has been acquired to enlarge other farms. The number of small-scale commercial farms—those with sales amounting to $250 to $1,200 a year—has showed the sharpest drop; but these have the least importance from the point of view of productivity. However, the number of large-scale commercial farms has showed a marked rise—although, significantly, only a small number of these are run by corporations or hired managers.

The trend of rising productivity in agriculture is continuing, and is likely to result in increasing production despite a continuing decline in the number of agricultural workers. The decline in the relative importance of agricultural employment began even before the Civil War, and has continued into the twentieth century. During the past twenty-five years, while farm production increased by more than one-half, the employed labor force on farms decreased by 35 percent, and the decline probably will continue into the future. This is expected even though, with the continued growth of population in the United

Table II

Index of Trends in Number of Farms in the United States

Category	1930	1940	1950	1954
All farms	100	97	86	76
Commercial farms	100	89	70	63
Large (class I, annual sales of $25,000 and over)	100	93	80	105
Medium (classes II through V, annual sales of $1,200 to $25,000)	100	85	66	63
Small (class VI, annual sales of $250 to $1,200)	100	110	89	58
Noncommercial farms (part-time and residential)	100	137	166	144

SOURCES: 1930-50—Ronald L. Mighell, *American Agriculture*, John Wiley and Sons, Inc., New York, 1955; 1954—Census of Agriculture, 1954, *op. cit.*

States, the demand for food will increase. For perhaps another decade, the rise in productivity, at least in certain agricultural staples, will exceed the rise in domestic demand. Moreover, much of the increase

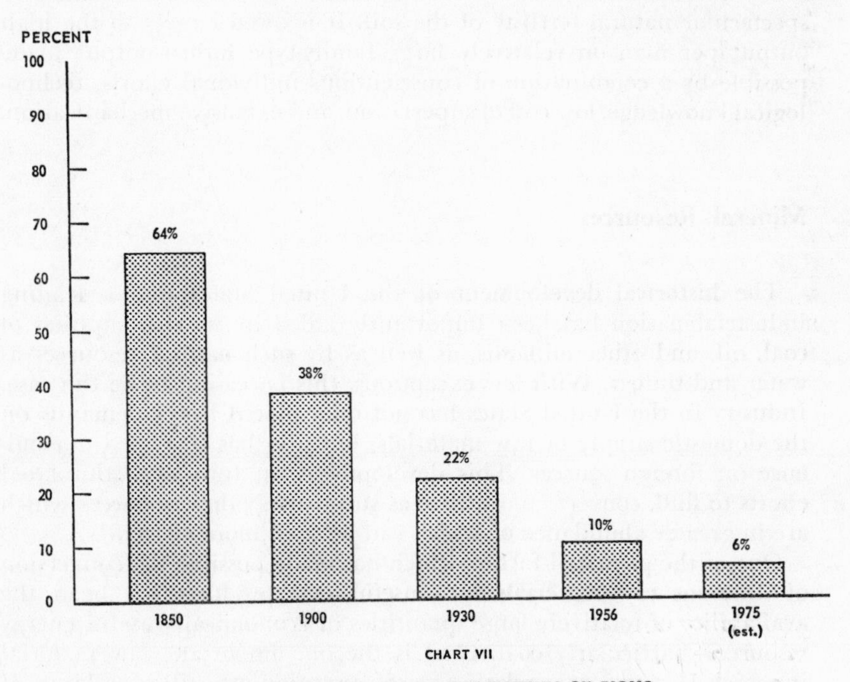

CHART VII

PERCENT OF LABOR FORCE WORKING ON FARMS

Source: 1850 - 1900 Statistical Abstract of the United States, 1957.
1930 - 1956 Economic Indicators - Historical Supplement, 1957.
1975 John D. Black, 'Agriculture in the Nation's Economy,' American Economic Review, March 1956.

in demand will be for food of higher quality, and will require additional labor for food processing, packing, and distribution rather than for farm work as such. Thus, a further reduction in the number and percentage of people working on farms is indicated.

Despite the lower level of agricultural productivity relative to nonagricultural activities, the output of the people working on American farms exceeds the demands of our own very high domestic consumption. It is a strange fact that the United States, one of the most highly industrialized countries of the world, should also have an exportable surplus of farm products—amounting to roughly 10 percent of its agricultural production. Such a large capacity for agricultural production was very important after each of the two World Wars, when serious food shortages occurred in various parts of the world. Its importance could continue if, with a rising world population, food deficiencies should create a serious problem in any of the more densely populated countries.

In summary, then, the high productivity of American agriculture today is not primarily the result of an unusually favorable climate or a spectacular natural fertility of the soil. It is owed largely to the high output per man on relatively large family-type farms—output made possible by a combination of conscientious individual efforts, technological knowledge, low cost of supervision, and extensive mechanization.

Mineral Resources

The historical development of the United States into a leading industrial nation has been importantly aided by its rich supplies of coal, oil, and other minerals, as well as by such natural resources as water and timber. With few exceptions, this is ceasing to be the case. Industry in the United States has not only placed heavy demands on the domestic supply of raw materials, but also has increased dependence on foreign sources. This development, in turn, has stimulated efforts to find, convert, and utilize as substitutes other resources which are in greater abundance or which can be used more efficiently.

One of the principal factors which has made possible the conversion of different raw materials into useful end products has been the availability of relatively large quantities of economically useful energy resources—particularly coal. Coal is the one important raw material in which U. S. reserves relative to consumption are still very large. If the rate of increase in fuel consumption of recent decades should continue, coal would be available in adequate amounts in the United States for a hundred years or longer, even though at somewhat rising real costs of production. The current output of coal in the United States is about 20 percent of world production, but reserves are estimated at one-third of the world's total.[2]

Energy from coal is probably cheaper in the United States than in most other parts of the world. Underground bituminous coal is mined at depths that rarely exceed 1,000 feet. In contrast, the average depth of mines in Great Britain and Japan is considerably more than 1,000 feet and some mines go down to a depth of 4,000 to 5,000 feet. Moreover, approximately one-fourth of American coal is produced in strip mines which do not require any underground operation. It is because of these benefits of nature and the high productivity in the mines that industry in many parts of the United States enjoys a considerable advantage over that of most other industrialized countries with respect to fuel cost.

The advantage of the United States in the cost of fuel, substantial as it is, does not appear so great if viewed in terms of total costs of producing manufactured goods. Other raw materials, labor, management, and capital must also be considered. In the manufacturing industry as a whole, fuel amounts roughly to 4 percent of the cost of processing the average product. In the industries where heat or power is used intensively, the effect of fuel costs naturally is greater. Furthermore, the availability of cheap sources of energy is likely to be of growing importance for further industrial development. With the world's rising population and advancing industrialization, more inroads are being made on the raw material resources of the globe. This requires the use of materials that are less accessible and of lower grades, and the gradual development of synthetic substitutes for natural raw materials. The processing of low-grade materials and the manufacture of synthetic substitutes, in turn, increase the use of energy per unit of output.

With the exception of coal and most agricultural raw materials, the current and the prospective rates of consumption of natural resources in the United States have outgrown the domestic supply base. Half a century ago, 15 percent of the nonagricultural raw materials produced in the United States were exported; today this percentage has been halved, and substantial and rising imports are now necessary. American industry during 1952 imported about 10 percent of its raw materials, excluding farm products and gold, and it is estimated that this dependence on foreign supply will rise to 20 percent within the next

---

[2]See *Report of the Panel on the Impact of the Peaceful Uses of Atomic Energy*, Joint Committee on Atomic Energy, Vol. 2, Washington, D. C., January 1956. In estimating useful reserves, coal supplies have been included which could be exploited if the price of coal (relative to other prices) were one and one-half times the present prices.

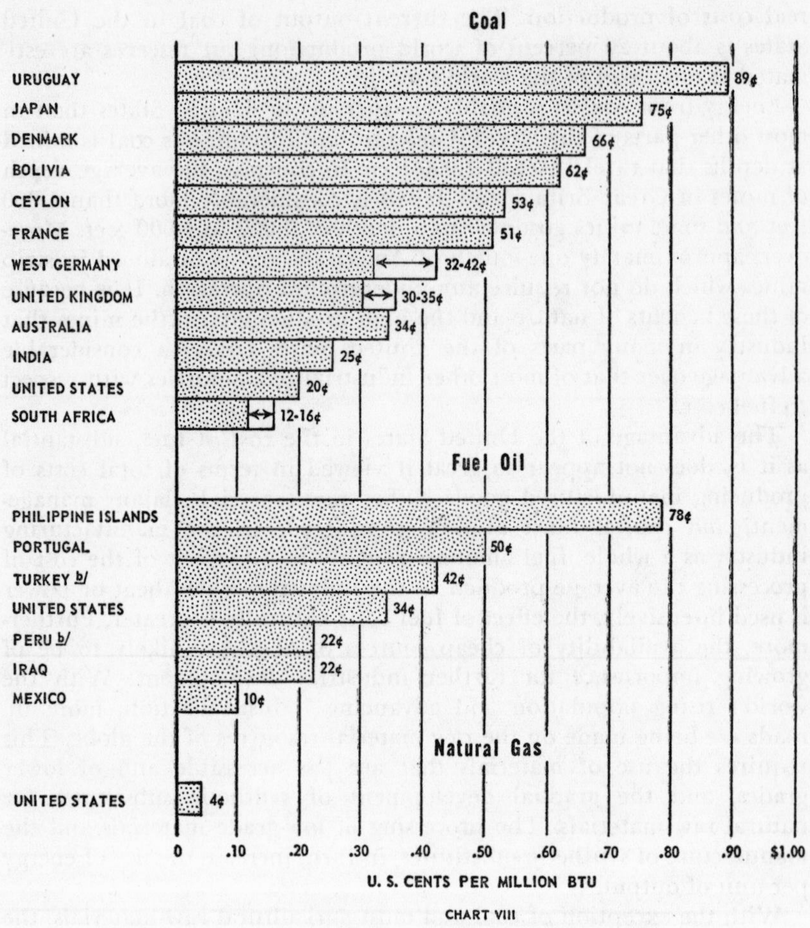

CHART VIII

FUEL COSTS IN SELECTED COUNTRIES a/, 1952

a/ Costs for the United States are for Pittsburgh (coal), Boston (fuel oil), Corpus Christi (natural gas); for Uruguay - Montevideo; for Philippines - Manilla; for United Kingdom - Edinburgh; for Australia - Newcastle; and for South Africa - Johannesburgh.

b/ 1953.

Source: Teitelbaum, P.D., International Fuel Costs, Staff paper, Productive Uses of Nuclear Energy Project, National Planning Association, Washington, D.C., August 1955, as reprinted in Report of the Panel on the Impact of the Peaceful Uses of Atomic Energy, Joint Committee on Atomic Energy, Vol. 2, January 1953, p.58.

two decades.[8] The particular import items which account for more than 50 percent of the total U. S. supply are too numerous to list. A few selected examples are given in Table III.

[8] *Resources for Freedom*, a Report by the President's Materials Policy Commission, Vol. 1, Washington, D. C., 1952, p. 2.

Table III

U. S. Imports of Selected Raw Materials as a Percent of Total Available Supply—1955

Raw Materials	Percent	Raw Materials	Percent
Food Products		Wood and Paper	
Bananas	100	Cork, unmanufactured	100
Coffee	100	Newsprint	78
Tea	100	Nonferrous Ores and Metals	
Tuna fish	56	Tin	100
Crude Rubber, Gums, and Resins		Nickel	97
Lac and shellac	100	Bauxite and aluminum	76
Rubber, natural	100	Lead	56
Vegetable Products		Zinc	52
Copra and coconut oil	100	Nonmetallic Minerals	
Quebracho extract	100	Mica	96
Textile Fibers		Asbestos	94
Jute	100	Fluorspar	57
Raw silk	100	Ferrous Ores and Metals	
Sisal and manila	100	Chrome	92
Cotton, long staple	58	Manganese ore	88
Wool, unmanufactured	56	Tungsten	57

SOURCES: *Contribution of Imports to United States Food Supplies*, U. S. Department of Commerce, November 1956; *Contribution of Imports to United States Raw Material Supplies*, U. S. Department of Commerce, January 1957.

One other natural resource, which in the past was available in great abundance in the United States, has become of increasing concern. The present rate at which water is used for irrigation, as well as for personal and industrial consumption, cannot be maintained in an expanding economy without making better provision for its efficient use. This will involve heavy new investments for the treatment and recovery of used water, the transportation of water over considerable distances, or, in future decades, the use of desalted brackish or sea water. Unfortunately, the impending problem of water utilization is not yet receiving the attention it deserves.

Historically, America's diverse and rich natural resources attracted many immigrants to its shores and these resources were among the factors which made possible the rapid rate of economic development. The surge of industrialization in the United States utilized nature's bounty in producing new products and providing for a higher standard of living. Nevertheless, while the country has been blessed with raw materials, the depletion of these mineral resources, except for coal, gives little advantage to American processing industries compared with those of other countries. And, as consumption per capita of world population increases, the demand for raw materials will rise. Were it not for the hope that suitable substitutes will be developed to serve the purpose of the scarcer minerals, the outlook for the future supply of some of the important industrial raw materials would be bleak indeed.

The high productivity of the American economy, it seems clear, cannot be attributed primarily to a favorable climate, extraordinary fertility of the soil, or abundance of mineral and other nonagricultural resources. Ample resources help, but only in combination with other factors.

Chapter III

Labor

PEOPLE are the greatest economic asset of any nation; the adequacy of natural resources has meaning only in relation to them. Progress and growth are more likely to take place if available population and natural resources are developed in approximate balance.

The United States has been fortunate in that nature provided resources for the support of an expanding population. As industrialization created increasing job opportunities, a large number of immigrants came from all parts of the world ready to offer their labor and skills in this new country. Thus, the growth of the labor force on the one hand, combined with the development of natural resources and of industry on the other hand, have contributed to the high level of per capita income in the United States.

Table IV

Population Density and National Income Per Capita

Country	Density of population[1]	National income per capita[2] (U. S. dollars)
United States	54	1,870
Canada	5	1,310
Switzerland	313	1,010
Australia	3	950
United Kingdom	544	780
France	205	740
Netherlands	857	500
Cuba	132	310
Italy	412	310
South Africa	28	300
Brazil	18	230
Mexico	39	220
Turkey	80	210
Japan	621	190
Philippines	192	150
Ceylon	339	110
India	300	60
Burma	75	50

[1] Population per square mile of area as of 1955.

[2] Average, 1952-54. Comparisons of per capita national income (or net national product) are only rough approximations of levels of personal income or personal welfare.

SOURCES: Population Density—*Statistical Yearbook 1956*, 8th issue, United Nations, Dept. of Economics and Social Affairs, New York, 1956; *Per Capita National Product of Fifty-five Countries, 1952-54*, United Nations, Statistical Papers, Series E No. 4, 1957.

Where population presses against limited or inadequately developed natural resources, a low level of per capita production and consumption results—a major difficulty of most Asian countries, for example. But low per capita income also exists where large sections of a country, though capable of development, are sparsely inhabited—as in parts of Latin America and West Africa. In some industrially advanced countries of Europe, where development has outgrown the domestic food and raw material base, a high per capita income results largely from a capacity to process imported raw materials into finished goods, many of which have, in turn, to be exported.

Composition of the Labor Force

The population of the United States now numbers more than 172 million and has been increasing in recent years at an annual rate of 1.8 percent. In 1957, the active civilian labor force in the United States totaled more than 68 million, of which about 46 million were men and 22 million were women. Approximately 30 percent of civilian manpower resources is employed in manufacturing industries; 20 percent in distributive, wholesale, and retail trades; 10 percent in agriculture; another 10 percent in government service; and about 30 percent in mining, construction, and other occupations.

Although the working age of the labor force extends from less than sixteen to over sixty-five years, the great bulk of the labor force is composed of workers twenty to sixty years old. The evils of child labor have been virtually abolished in the United States. This has been brought about not only through legislation but also through the fact that most states require regular attendance at school for children until the age of fifteen or sixteen. Thus, the employment of young people is generally limited to part-time jobs during the school year and full-time employment during summer vacations. At the opposite end of the age scale, greater provision for personal security—old-age assistance, pension plans, and private insurance—has permitted many older workers to retire. However, this is not an unmixed blessing. In some cases, people of advanced age feel that the retirement necessary to obtain old-age benefits deprives them of an opportunity to work while they still enjoy vigorous health. American employment practices have not yet been adjusted to the achievements of the medical sciences in prolonging the period during which the individual is capable of productive work.

One distinctive characteristic of the American labor force is its heterogeneity. Originally composed of immigrants, a substantial part of the American population has continued to be made up of immigrants and their sons and daughters. Although legislation since the 1920's has greatly restricted large-scale immigration to America, the foreign-born population and their American-born children still accounted in 1950 for one-fourth of the total white population and constituted almost a third of the white labor force (see Appendix Table 7). Although population heterogeneity is not peculiar to the United States, its contribution to economic development has been particularly significant. Immigrants from different countries and cultural backgrounds brought a great variety of aptitudes and skills, and a determination to make a place for themselves in a new land.

A second characteristic of the American labor force which has contributed to high productivity grows out of the fact that the United States extends across a large part of a continent. A traveler can cover the 2,500 miles from New York to San Francisco without once crossing national boundaries. In contrast, a traveler covering approximately the same mileage in Europe—say from Lisbon to Moscow—would have to cross seven national boundaries, use eight different currencies, and nowadays would have to pierce an "Iron Curtain" in the process.

This continent-wide area of the United States has facilitated greater mobility of the population and the labor force than has been possible in Europe. It has also provided new areas for settlement as the population grew and the economy expanded. In Europe, changes in the distribution of the population over past decades largely reflect higher rates of natural population growth in Eastern Europe. In contrast, changes in the distribution of population in the United States have largely been caused by internal migration.

This high degree of geographical mobility has been matched in the United States by a great deal of occupational mobility. Characteristically, Americans have never acknowledged a moral, social, or economic pressure to continue in the occupations of their fathers. Opportunities have existed for people to change jobs, and American custom has always strongly sanctioned the practice of occupational mobility. This attitude has made it easy for the American labor force to shift from less productive industries and lower-wage occupations to those with higher rates of output and higher pay scales. The greater mobility of labor helps to explain why American productivity may increase more rapidly than in some other countries where similar technological methods exist.

The disparity in productivity between American workers and those in some other countries does not result from innate differences in abilities. Each nation has its own special historical or geographical circumstances which explain the distinguishing aptitudes or skills of its labor force. Maritime people, like those of Scandinavia, become

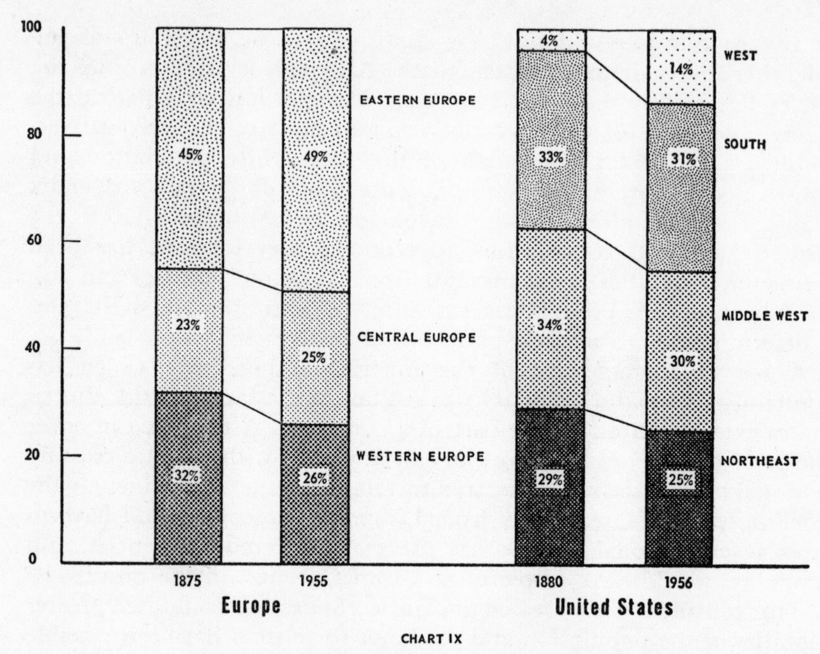

CHART IX

POPULATION DISTRIBUTION - EUROPE and UNITED STATES
(percent of total)

Sources: Europe - U.N. Demographic Yearbook, 1952; U.N. Statistical Yearbook, 1956.
United States - Statistical Abstract, 1957; Census Bureau, Current Population Reports, Series P-25 No. 165, November 4, 1957.

great sailors and fishermen because they are near the sea and need to supplement the slender resources of their land as population increases. Also, it is as natural for the peasant of the Ukraine to grow wheat as it is for the Kansas farmer, since the flat plains and continental climates of both regions are admirably suited for the production of this crop.

Health and Training of American Workers

A good diet and good living conditions, with plenty of fresh air and recreation during childhood and youth, are probably the most important factors making for a good physical constitution in the mature worker. Enormous advances have been made in recent decades in developing more adequate diets, in providing more healthful living conditions and medical care for Americans of all age groups. The resulting improvements in physical strength and stamina have contributed substantially to the rise in workers' productivity in the United States.

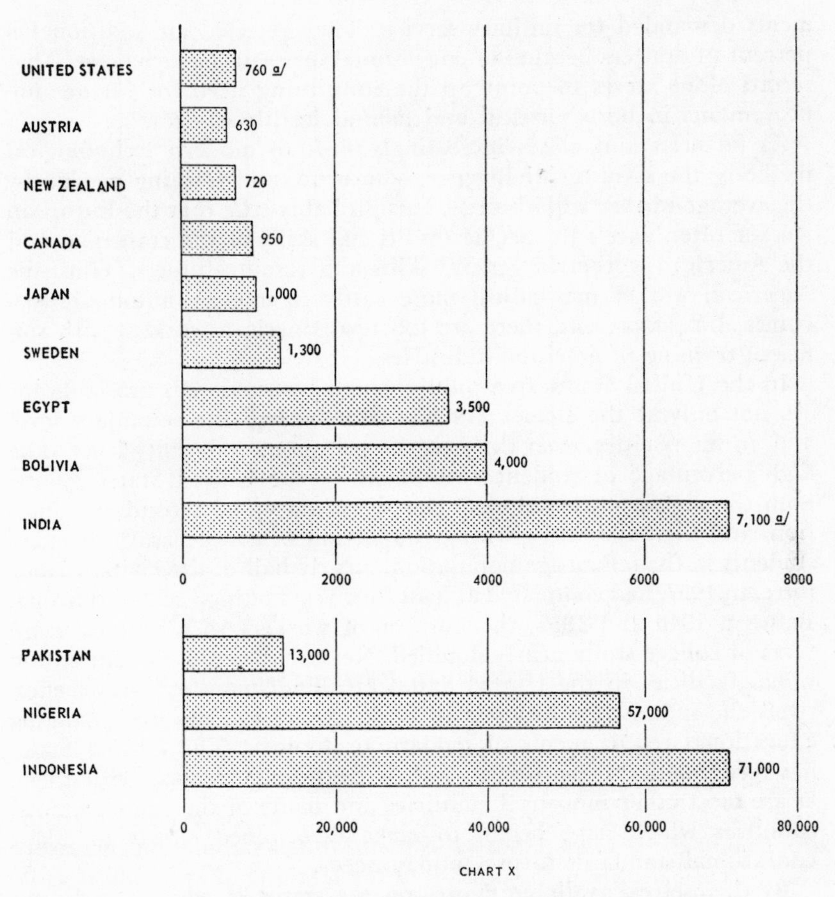

CHART X

NUMBER OF INHABITANTS PER PHYSICIAN, 1954

a/ 1953.

Source: United Nations Statistical Yearbook, 1956.

Nonetheless, these advances should not hide the fact that there is ample room for improvement in the present status of American health. The estimate that, on the average, about 2 percent of all potential man-days are lost through temporary nonoccupational accidents or sickness, indicates the continuing need to improve medical care and research. Another aspect of health which has been receiving greater, though still insufficient, attention in recent years concerns mental health—the problem of developing healthy psychological personalities as well as healthy bodies. In the United States during World War II, the Armed Forces rejected more than 25 percent of all draftees examined for duty because they did not meet minimum physical requirements demanded for military service. They rejected an additional 5 percent of draftees because of educational or mental deficiencies. That record alone serves to point up the continuing need for further improvements in both physical and mental health services.

As factories and offices increasingly shift to modern technological methods, the level of intelligence, education, and training needed by the average worker will also rise. It is probably true that the European worker often excels in specific traditional skills of the craftsman and the American worker in general skills and resourcefulness. Thus, the American worker may adjust more easily to modern automatic machines; but at present, there are too few American workers with sufficient training in precision industries.

In the United States, free public school instruction is available for all, not only at the elementary but also through the secondary level and, in many cities, even through the college or university level. The high percentage of student enrollment in the United States reflects both the almost universal character of primary and secondary education, and the large and growing proportion of college and university students in the school-age population. Nearly half of the civilian labor force, in 1957, had completed at least four years of high school training. Between 1940 and 1957, the number of workers with four or more years of college study nearly doubled. Nevertheless, the present educational facilities in the United States are inadequate to handle effectively the increased enrollment of students and to meet the changing educational requirements of modern technology. The United States has recognized these problems and is beginning to cope with them, as are most other industrial countries and many of the less developed countries which have begun to make determined efforts to adapt educational standards to present-day needs.

By themselves, available figures on the status of education do not give an altogether clear comparison of the training received by workers in various countries (see Appendix Table 8). In many parts of Europe, for example, the formal educational training of the prospective worker ends at the age of fourteen or fifteen, after about eight to nine years of schooling. Since most secondary schools are on a tuition basis, many students enter the labor force at the completion of their elementary school training. However, because of the lack of sufficient technical instruction at the elementary school level, many countries provide extensive apprenticeship periods and vocational training classes in order to develop those technical skills which contribute to a more productive labor force.

In Germany, for example, technical institutes *(Fachschulen)* have been established to provide advanced training and education for the mature apprentice or journeyman. In England, junior technical schools prepare young workers for specific industries and occupations.

In the Soviet Union, specialized schools *(technikums)* have been set up which offer a four-year course in general and special training. These schools extend educational training beyond the minimum provided by public education, and offer extended academic and technical instruction. The vocational training schools and apprenticeship programs in Europe are primarily concerned with increasing the force of skilled workers and semi-professional technicians needed for efficient operation and maintenance of the complex equipment in today's factories. They have no exact counterpart in the educational system or vocational training programs in the United States.

In the United States, on-the-job training programs are relied upon very heavily to provide young workers with technical experience and to supplement the training acquired through vocational or occupational schools. Many factories and organizations have established special training programs which prepare workers for their new assignments. These are not considered as extracurricular programs but are conducted as an integral part of the worker's indoctrination in the job itself. The primary objective of on-the-job training, however, is not to produce a staff of semi-professional technicians, as do the *technikums* or *Fachschulen*. Rather, it familiarizes the new worker with the tasks he is expected to perform and with the general operations of the plant or firm. The more widespread development of mechanization and automation and the growing demand for repair and maintenance workers in the United States are likely to result also in an increased emphasis on the type of technical training which goes beyond today's vocational training but requires less than a full engineering course.

Thus, while the American labor force may be healthier and may receive more formal education than the labor force in many other countries, it is doubtful that differences in physical stamina and in schooling and training explain the extraordinarily high labor productivity in the United States compared with that elsewhere. Other factors must be more important in explaining the difference.

Labor's Attitudes

In the United States, there is no single attitude which is typical of labor as a whole, but rather a variety of attitudes on the part of various groups. Differences exist between the views and opinions of recent immigrants and those of American-born workers, between labor in one region and labor in another region, between white and nonwhite workers, and so on. Nevertheless, certain general characteristics of American labor attitudes can be distinguished. Most of these are revealed in the American workers' views of the purpose and functions of trade unions.[1]

In a labor force of 68 million workers, close to 18 million Americans are union members. In manufacturing industry, however, union members make up about half of the employed labor force. The typical American trade union is an organization established and maintained for the primary purpose of obtaining higher wages and improved labor conditions. They are wholly independent organizations, and are not sponsored or controlled by government or employers.

In other countries, particularly in Central Europe, the development of trade unions was historically only one part of a more general labor movement—of which political parties, consumer cooperatives, and often cultural and sports organizations were other parts. Such comprehensive labor movements abroad were responses to the fact that workers regarded themselves—and were regarded by others—as members of a distinct class which did not share the blessings of society with the so-called "upper" classes and who, therefore, had to develop their own cultural and economic life.

In contrast, the American worker does not regard himself as a member of a distinct class set apart from other classes in the nation. As a worker, he has special interests which he wants to see actively furthered by a strong and powerful labor organization. But, aside from these immediate concerns, as in the case of other Americans, the worker's choice of a political party, church, and other organizations does not rest on his particular occupation and economic status. National and cultural origin, religious affiliation, regional and local loyalties, and other common interests have created in the United States stronger social ties among people than any concept of economic class, defined by the position a man holds in the process of production.

Although the American worker does not regard the labor movement as an all-embracing way of life, he does expect his union to fight hard for his economic interests. Since the 1930's, there has been a tremendous growth in union membership, and unions have made substantial gains for workers in the form of more wages, leisure time, and various types of fringe benefits. Though the average American worker achieves far more than a minimum subsistence living standard, he is still very responsive to the prospect of greater material rewards. He works overtime when he has the opportunity to do so, because he may earn 50 percent more for overtime work than for regular work. In some industries where the average work week has been reduced to 35 hours,

---

[1]For an elaboration of labor's attitudes toward unionism see James B. Carey, Clinton S. Golden, Marion H. Hedges, Eric Peterson, and Arnold S. Zander, *Trade Unions and Democracy—A Comparative Study of U. S., French, Italian, and West German Unions,* PP 100, National Planning Association, Washington, 1957.

many workers have accepted additional part-time employment even though their primary jobs provide an adequate income.

Labor-management disputes exist in the United States as in all countries in which the workers are free to seek their own betterment. As labor relations has improved over the last two decades, day-to-day collective bargaining has resolved the vast majority of differences between management and workers. This does not mean that strikes have not been frequent, but that they have been conducted with far less bitterness and violence than in the early days of the union movement. Work stoppages resulting from labor-management disputes caused an average loss of one-half of one percent of total man-days worked in the United States during the years 1950-54. The situation in the United States is not unusual in this respect (see Appendix Table 9). In some countries where labor is free to strike, the number of working days lost as a result of work stoppages has been as high as in the United States; in other countries, less.

American workers regard management as the opposite party in the labor contract and fight hard to obtain the most favorable terms for themselves. But, they also recognize a basic community of interest with management and realize that only a prosperous enterprise can afford to pay high wages and other labor benefits. Recognizing the value of such an attitude, management invests considerable effort and money in creating and maintaining pleasant working conditions. A large and growing number of factories are increasing output per worker through continuous improvement in the physical and psychological conditions of work. In response, workers in many plants have developed a pride of workmanship in a good product, and in many cases have taken an active and constructive interest in instituting management improvements. A series of NPA case studies[2] reported that an attitude of mutual interest and cooperation on the parts both of management and labor not only helped to resolve disputes through peaceful collective bargaining procedures, but also tended to increase worker productivity by encouraging labor to take a more active interest in improving productive operations.

Although many unions have been active in urging the adoption of new techniques and in facilitating introduction of more efficient methods in using labor, improving training methods, making better assignments of labor, and providing better supervision of employees' work, the attitudes in a few trade unions are still hindering the elimination of wasteful practices. For example, some unions still attempt

---

[2]See *Causes of Industrial Peace under Collective Bargaining,* edited by Clinton S. Golden and Virginia D. Parker for the National Planning Association, Harper & Brothers, New York, 1955.

to restrict the entry of newcomers into their trades; and "featherbedding" adds to employment in some industries without a compensating increase in output. During the period of large-scale unemployment in the 1930's particularly, such wasteful and antiquated practices plagued the building construction, transportation, and entertainment industries. However, under the conditions of high employment in the past decade, such practices have been diminishing, even though they have not entirely disappeared.

On the whole, American labor has come to realize that increases in productivity not only make possible increases in real wages but are also necessary in order to sustain economic growth. Nonetheless, union leaders have legitimately and consistently insisted that management and government policies be designed to mitigate the hardships of shifts in employment resulting from such technological advances as well as to promote full employment. Trade union representatives from foreign countries who have visited the United States have repeatedly expressed their astonishment at this positive attitude of American labor towards technological advances, including the most recent adoption of automation.

In summary, then, the rise in the productivity of American labor is not merely the result of special historical and geographical circumstances affecting the workers' heterogeneity and mobility. It depends also upon the physical stamina of the labor force, the education and training of the workers, and their attitudes toward work, leisure, and innovations. These attitudes of American labor are among the significant factors contributing to the high output per man-hour in American industry. But, regardless of their significance, these characteristics of American workers alone do not explain the differences in productivity among the various countries.

Chapter IV

Business Management

NO OTHER ASPECT of American economic life has undergone more basic changes during the last half century than the role and character of business management. This transformation undoubtedly has been a major factor in the rapid rise in American productivity. It is perhaps significant that the leaders of Soviet Russia have repeatedly emphasized that communism could learn a great deal from the ways in which production is managed in the United States. At the same time, they have never ceased to repeat the Marxist dogma that the "anarchic" organization of production is bound to lead, through crisis after crisis, to the eventual doom of the capitalistic system.

An accurate appraisal of the place of business management in American economic and social life is difficult because different types of management exist side by side. Today, there are still some businesses which are being operated very much as they were over a century ago. A sizable number of concerns are still owned and managed by the children or grandchildren of their founders. But there is a marked trend toward management by executives trained in the application of new business methods and technology.

During the second half of the nineteenth century, many entrepreneurs broke through the family patterns of ownership and management, and created great business empires in railroads, steel, copper, lumber, oil, urban real estate, banking, shipping, and retail trade. These were the "rugged individualists," often ruthless in the competitive struggle, who amassed fortunes, frequently engaged in monopolistic practices, and became targets of popular criticism. This criticism was particularly articulate during the latter decades of the nineteenth century and the early decades of the twentieth century, when the enrichment of these so-called "robber barons" and their conspicuous consumption were in stark contrast to the lot of farmers suffering from low agricultural prices and of immigrant labor suffering from low wages and bad and insecure working conditions. Popular criticism of the great industrial empires resulted in the adoption of antitrust laws and other regulative measures. While such legislation halted many objectionable practices, it did not halt the contributions made to the development of the American economy by the building of these industrial and financial enterprises. The imaginative genius and passionate self-interest of many of these men had creative as well as negative aspects. They helped to transform a nation of small farmers, aristocratic plantation owners, and small-scale artisans into a great and wealthy industrial power of continental scope and worldwide significance.

Oddly enough, some discussion of modern business management tacitly assumes that we are still dealing with those nineteenth-century robber barons. Nor is it only the Marxist critics of the present American economic system who write and speak in this way. The same error—though for opposite reasons—is made by some panegyrists of the American economy when they continue to celebrate the self-centered aggressiveness of these vanished rugged individualists, whose present-day managerial successors have acquired quite different standards of organizational conformity, social responsibility, and concern for public opinion.

The Characteristics of Small and Large Business

A casual observer of the contemporary American scene could easily get the impression that the giant corporation is predominant in production and distribution. More careful investigation shows that, though the giant corporation is important, it is not dominant. For the tax year ending June 1955, there were in the United States over 700,000 corporations filing tax returns, of which about 1,700 had assets of $50 million and more. These 1,700 largest corporations accounted for about 60 percent of both total assets and total net income, but only 38 percent of gross sales of all American corporations. While these figures show the importance of the 1,700 biggest corporations, they also show the large number of corporations which do not belong to the class of giants.

The American dream envisages a society in which an energetic and resourceful individual with talent and courage can establish himself in business and become his own boss. Today, it is virtually impossible for any one person to obtain the resources necessary to start a steel plant, an automobile factory, or an oil refinery. There are, nevertheless, ample opportunities for establishing small or medium-sized businesses in other branches of industry, trade, and services. Although statistics are not entirely conclusive on this point, opportunities for small business ventures do not appear to have diminished in recent decades.

Statistics of profitability, however, show that the smaller corporations are more sensitive to economic fluctuations than the very large corporations, and that the smaller corporations have a lower rate of

Table V

Corporation Tax Returns by Asset Classes, Tax Year 1954-55

	Number of returns (Thous.)	Number of returns (%)	Total assets (%)	Total receipts (%)	Net income (%)
Returns with balance sheets:					
Assets under $1 million........	618.3	85.5	10.0	27.6	9.1
Assets $1 to $50 million........	47.8	6.6	29.5	33.4	29.2
Assets $50 million and over.....	1.7	.2	60.5	37.6	61.1
Total........................	667.8	92.4	100.0	98.6	99.4
Returns with no balance sheets..	55.0	7.6	—	1.4	.6
Total corporation tax returns...	722.8	100.0	100.0	100.0	100.0

SOURCES: *Statistics of Income for 1954*, U. S. Treasury Department, Washington, D. C., 1957.

profits as measured by earnings on invested capital or per share of stock. These lower profits must be attributed, at least in part, to the fact that the owners of smaller corporations often receive profits in the form of managerial salaries for themselves or members of their families rather than as dividends on stocks.

There has been much debate as to whether the large or small concern is more efficient. It has been recognized generally that the larger corporations can more easily obtain necessary financing and are better able to pay for expensive research and development projects and for advertising. Offsetting these advantages, however, is the often expressed opinion that large corporations are bureaucratic and suffer from inflexibility. Some people have even maintained that the managers of large corporations shy away from new ventures involving risks because they are afraid of being criticized by their boards of directors in the event of failure. These opinions need to be examined in the light of actual American experience.

The difficulties of small and medium-sized businesses in the last few years certainly substantiate the claim that they are less able to obtain needed financing than are the large corporations, particularly in periods of tight credit. Lending institutions, especially banks, are naturally inclined to give preference to the larger borrowers with long-established lines of credit and substantial assets. Aside from this, however, the disadvantage of smaller enterprises reflects the fact that such companies do not have sufficient funds available from the internal sources of capital—depreciation accruals, undistributed profits, etc.—whereas much of the financing needs of large corporations can be readily satisfied from these sources.

Bureaucratic inflexibility and timidity are not as general in large corporations as is often imagined. During the past decade, many big corporations have been reasonably successful in devising methods of decentralizing decision making and delegating authority—for example, the General Electric Company—and even in developing competition among their component divisions—as in the General Motors Corporation. Finally, many of the most novel and imaginative ventures in recent years have been the work of large corporations. Transistors, for example, were invented in the laboratory of a large corporation; production methods, however, have been developed and carried out by both large and small companies as licensees of the original inventor.

Certain characteristics of small businesses tend to offset the advantages of the large corporations. The more outstanding small corporations have owed their success and ability to compete with larger

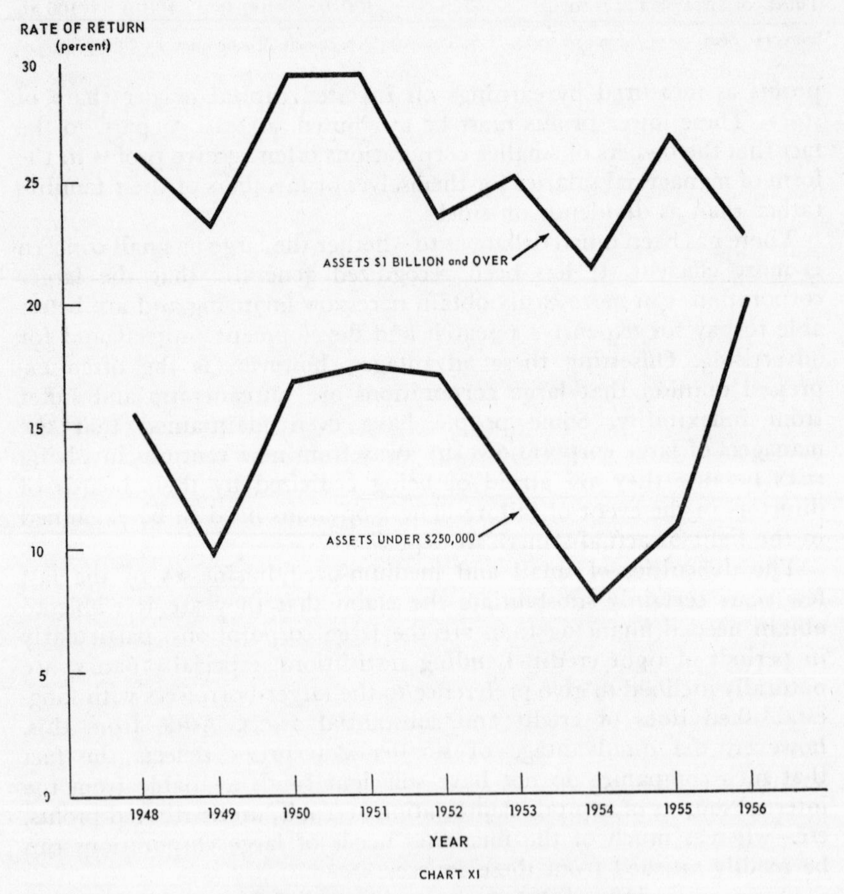

CHART XI

AVERAGE ANNUAL RATE OF RETURN BEFORE TAXES -
U. S. Manufacturing Corporations by Asset Size
(profits as a percent of stockholder's equity)

Source: See Appendix Table 10.

and wealthier rivals to flexible operations and versatile management. Small companies have been in the forefront of technological advance in many of the newer industrial fields—for example, electronics, automation equipment, certain components and materials for guided missiles, and other types of national defense work. Furthermore, new developments, such as tape-controlled machine tools and less expensive electronic computers, increasingly are bringing automation within reach of small businesses. Where the availability of financing, research, and advertising is not important, the difference in size is not the determining factor in the relative competitive ability of small and large corporations.

While the existence of large and small business units side by side was not the sole cause of rising productivity, it was a factor without which the spectacular rise would not have taken place. This consideration is not intended to imply that the existing mixture of large and small enterprises in the United States is the best possible one. Nor should the possibility be overlooked that, through use of its financial superiority, a large corporation might deliberately hinder the development of smaller companies, which in all other respects might be competitive. Here, we are primarily interested in the effect of the large corporations on the productivity of the American economy. This effect undoubtedly has been positive.

The Extent of Competition

The fear that, with the growth of large enterprises, competition would be replaced by monopoly has not materialized. Giant corporations in the American economy are larger than those in other industrial nations simply because American industry serves a larger market. Yet, despite—or partly because of—the importance of corporations which serve a continent-wide market, there is probably more competition among American producers than in any other country.

Sometimes overlooked are the differences in the methods of competition in industries with a few dominant producers and those in which there are hundreds or thousands of small producers. Competition among the few can be very keen. Moreover, competition among producers of the same product, in many instances, is supplemented by rivalry between products serving essentially the same purpose—between cotton and synthetic fibers, for example. It is paradoxical that in certain fields the spread of large enterprises has resulted in substantially greater competition than when the market was served by many small business units. This has been particularly true in the retail field, and has been fostered by the mobility of consumers resulting from the automobile and by the spread of shopping by telephone and mail.

Before the rise of chainstores and mail order and discount houses, and the practice of national advertising, many small specialized retail shops relied upon locational advantages and established custom in their competition with one another rather than upon differences in prices, quality, credit terms, and so on. This is still the situation in many countries. But in the United States today, there is much keener price competition among, for example, the large food store chains—Safeway, A & P, and others—than ever existed among their innumerable small predecessors. Such price competition is made possible by large sales volumes and has resulted in low profit margins. It has brought to consumers wider choices of goods and increases in shopping conveniences and services at lower costs.

In other fields as well, advancing technology and the maintenance of competitive conditions have exerted a downward pressure on prices. Automobiles and television sets are leading examples. In these fields, technological advances encourage formation of larger enterprises, and increased size leads to a relative increase in overhead costs. The costs of engineering, capital equipment, advertising, and general administration account for a rising share of total costs, while those of raw materials and labor for direct production take a lower share. This creates a powerful incentive for businesses to maintain a high rate of operation, even at reduced prices. Every product sold at a price above the out-of-pocket costs for current production adds to the total gain or reduces the total loss. In the light of these incentives, it is perhaps surprising that prices are not drastically reduced to the point of chaos as soon as some excess capacity appears. The explanation lies in the fact that, in determining price policy, management considers not only the immediate effect of maximum return (or minimum loss) but also the long-run effect. A firm is interested in maintaining a price which exceeds both variable and overhead costs while encouraging as many sales as possible over a period of time.

The existence of effective competition among large American corporations does not mean that there are no dangers of monopolistic price exploitation or that the need for a watchful antitrust policy can be ignored. Though most American economic activity—measured by either employment or output—is in decentralized and small and middle-sized industries, the degree of concentration in certain industries has become a matter of concern. Bigness—which we discuss in more detail in Chapter XI—means concentration of economic power, but this is not in itself necessarily an economic or social evil. Power can be used in a constructive way, just as it can be abused to the detriment of society.

The Changed Role of Management

One important safeguard against the misuse of power by big corporations has been the important changes during the past twenty years in the character of business management both in large and in small enterprises. It is not mere chance that in the business field we now hear little of the Rockefellers, Carnegies, Astors, and Vanderbilts, but a great deal about General Motors, General Electric, Standard Oil, and American Telephone and Telegraph. True, there are still some individuals who have amassed great fortunes; but, they are the exceptions, and with present income and estate tax rates they will probably remain exceptions. Today, most large business organizations are led by men hardly known by name to the general public.

The emergence of business management as a profession is probably one of the most important recent developments in the American economy. The members of this new profession are less colorful and less ruggedly individualistic than their predecessors. Typically, they are salaried employees of their corporations, not the owners. In recent decades, top management has been recruited increasingly from individuals with technical and marketing backgrounds rather than financial experience as in the past. Trained in schools of business administration, modern executives understand the value of applied science and technology—in the office as well as in the factory—in achieving efficiency, meeting competition, and offsetting rising costs of labor and materials. They are conscious of their responsibilities to stockholders, workers, customers, and—most of all—to the corporation itself as a permanent institution with a life of its own.

Within the corporation, management has become aware of the necessity for team work and cooperation, and of the importance of mutually beneficial relations with trade unions. Dependent for personal advancement upon their own reputations and prestige, today's managers readily appreciate the contribution which their corporation's reputation—among customers, competitors, and the public generally—makes to the improvement of sales and the recruitment of personnel. Making a "quick killing" has become much less important than ensuring, over the long term, both a respected and a profitable place for the company in its industry.

This heightened sense of the necessity for cooperative attitudes and socially responsible actions has not resulted in any decline in the entrepreneurial vigor of American business. Quite the contrary. American corporations are committed to mass production for mass consumption. This means large volumes with relatively small profit margins, and vigorous struggles to maintain and, if possible, increase the share of the national market captured by each corporation. It means large-scale and ingenious advertising and sales promotion campaigns. It means a constant search for improved or new products and novel distribution methods. Thus, far-flung markets, nation-wide advertising media, relatively high and widely distributed incomes, and large corporate units—all have combined to create conditions under which management must continually develop and improve production and marketing methods.

Another consequence of the evolution of the new group of corporate managers is the development of long-range program planning by business firms. Today, there is hardly a large corporation which does not have an economic research staff to analyze its market outlook within the prospect for the American economy as a whole. The resulting projections for long-range investment and shorter-range production and distribution serve as guides to major policy decisions by top management. In this way, the immediate interests and activities of the corporation are related to the general growth possibilities of the economy as a whole for a period of five to ten or even more years. These projections, together with a consideration of such other factors as financial capabilities, consideration of industrial specialization or diversification, personal preferences of executives and directors, etc., enter into business investment decisions. While the price signals of the market are still important, the reactions of businessmen to them are based more upon longer-term profit expectations and less upon immediate sales prospects than in the past.

A wide variety of firms in many different industries in recent years have adopted rather similar assumptions with respect to the growth prospects of the economy as a whole. This has introduced a measure of general compatibility in their investment programs. Such common agreement on the outlook for continued expansion has undoubtedly contributed to the high and generally rising level of business investments for expansion and modernization which, in turn, has helped to make possible rising productivity and the growth of the whole economy.

Other important characteristics of the new type of business management are its willingness to make adjustments to changing economic and social conditions and its practical approaches to such decisions. Management's readiness to cast off worn-out and rigid or abstract doctrinal principles has been a major factor in its capacity for rapid adjustment to the changing circumstances of the American economy as a whole. Management's willingness to develop and use new and more productive methods in factory and office is reflected in its interest in training courses for executives and in its promotion of schools of engineering, technology, and business administration. But, education and training will add to productivity only if there is something worthwhile to teach and to learn. Hence, scientific and technological research have been indispensable factors in the growth of productivity.

Without them, even the best business management could not have accomplished the results achieved.

With the evolution of the corporation as an important institution in American social and economic life, the art of business management has advanced almost as much as has technology in the factory. There is increasing recognition of the significance of the attitudes and methods of the new group of corporate managers for the achievements of the American economy.

Chapter V

Research and Technology

THE AMERICAN PHILOSOPHER George Santayana went deeper than the proverb "necessity is the mother of invention" to point out that abundance should be called the mother of invention. Peoples who barely subsist under heavy pressure from their physical or economic environments, with a meager stock of ideas and tools, advance slowly, if at all. Hence, most of the original advances of civilization took place in the lush river valleys of Asia and Africa, while tribes who never knew where or when they would next eat rarely progressed beyond the most primitive stages of culture. Certainly, abundance has been one of the primary causes as well as one of the major consequences of America's achievements in research and technology.

Applied and Basic Sciences

No modern industrial country monopolizes talent and accomplishments in either the basic or applied sciences. But Americans have been particularly outstanding in applying the results of basic scientific research and in technological innovation—whether based on domestic or foreign inventions. Some discoveries originally developed outside the United States found their first practical applications in America because the markets of the countries of origin were too small and noncompetitive to warrant expenditures on frequent improvements in products and production methods. For example, several of the most important inventions in the automotive field have been made in Western Europe, but some were adapted to practical uses by American automobile manufacturers a decade or more before similar commercial applications by the German, British, or French producers who had developed the original ideas or prototypes.

This propensity to innovate is the key element in the relationship between American productivity and scientific research and application. Today, the benefits from this relationship extend well beyond industry and agriculture. The physician and dentist with their modern instruments, the laundryowner with his automatic clothes washers, dryers, and ironers, and the housewife with her vacuum cleaner and electric dishwasher—these and scores of other Americans are continually benefiting from scientific and technological advances in industry.

Moreover, modern research and technology reach beyond the physical processes of production to affect business organization and administration. Even before the introduction of mass production techniques in American industry, it was known that efficient organization of the production process could increase productivity just as could the introduction of new tools and machines. Somewhat later, it was recognized that pleasant working conditions increased human efficiency and decreased friction in the productive process. In recent years, research studies by both management and labor have contributed to the general acceptance and application of these principles and to the subsequent increase in productivity.

Despite their importance for productivity, to date, the progress in the social sciences has been more difficult to achieve than in the physical sciences. In part, this arises from the nature of the social sciences—the multiplicity of factors involved, the limited scope for controlled experimentation, and the virtual impossibility of eliminating value judgments. However, the difficulty also results from inadequate financial support of the social sciences from both private and governmental sources.

The economic and social applications of scientific and technological research are dependent upon more fundamental discoveries of science. Most of the great basic discoveries in physics, chemistry, and the life sciences during the past three centuries have been made in Europe or by scientists trained in the European tradition.

This is not to say that Americans have not made significant contributions to philosophy and science. They have—ever since Benjamin Franklin provided proof that a talent for pure and applied science plus practical wisdom and statesmanship could be combined in one person. Or, to give another example, modern industrial technology rests on Eli Whitney's theoretical concept of interchangeable parts. However, during the last century, organized fundamental research has not been carried on as intensively in the United States as in European countries.

This lag reflects the differences in attitudes toward basic and applied research in America and in Europe. For example, appointment to the Académie des Sciences in France, or to its equivalents in the United Kingdom, Germany, and Russia (both under czarist and communist rule), constitutes the highest honor that could be bestowed upon men and women devoting their life to pure research. Thus, the goal of becoming an academician has provided a great stimulus to European scientific advancement. The corresponding institutions in America, however, have received much less recognition and support and have not attained the stature of their European counterparts. In Europe, scientists and teachers enjoy the kind of prestige that in America more often goes to the successful business executive, especially the self-made man.

In a recent report, the Council of the American Association for the Advancement of Science pointed out that "the progress of basic science (in the United States) does not appear to be keeping pace with the development of applied science." The major reason usually advanced for this neglect of fundamental research is the practical orientation, both of those who engage in and of those who finance scientific and technological investigations. During World War II, American scientists heeded the call of government to work on weapons development; after the war, many of the more talented scientists and engineers left. Among those trained in science, the most creative and successful researchers often prefer to work for industrial laboratories concentrating on applied sciences rather than for government, academic, or "pure" research institutions.

Today, less than 10 percent of all expenditures for research and development in the United States are being devoted to the investigation of the fundamental processes of nature and the formulation and testing of scientific hypotheses. The comparative lack of interest in fundamental research in the United States and the relatively meager funds used for this purpose have been a growing concern to American scientists and government officials.

In this situation, the dramatic advances of Russian scientific research demonstrated by the successful launching of artificial earth satellites have come as a shock to America, and have provided an additional impetus for a thorough re-examination of basic attitudes and of the system of education and research. This re-examination is likely to affect our educational system at all levels, from primary through high schools, vocational schools, and universities, and it probably will stimulate more fundamental research.

The belief in scientific and technological progress is so deeply engrained in the American people that the recognition of a serious deficiency in this field is a challenge which is not likely to be overlooked. There is a danger, however, that in the haste to correct this deficiency, Americans will concentrate too narrowly on technical education and training in the natural sciences and mathematics. Creative achievements in these fields depend not only on mastery of technique and detail but even more importantly upon the so-called theoretical and philosophical aspects of these sciences as well as upon the broad fertilizing influence of the culture as a whole. Where there is a rich and diversified cultural tradition which also values and supports the social sciences, arts, and humanities, the natural sciences—in both their technical and theoretical aspects—are creatively stimulated by new perspectives and by the perception of wider and deeper meanings. A balanced educational system, which emphasizes content as well as method and inculcates a love of learning for its own sake, is a necessary precondition for fruitful advances in basic and applied science, as it is in every field of intellectual endeavor. One result of such an improved educational system would be more rapid advances in industrial technology and rising productivity.

Personnel and Expenditures for Research

The fact that the United States now needs more scientific manpower should not obscure the fact that a growing number of Americans have been turning to scientific pursuits in recent decades. The number of scientists and engineers has increased since 1930 at a rate four times greater than the growth of the labor force (see Appendix Table 11). Most of the technicians in the American labor force are concerned with actual production work because the increasing complexity of production processes requires their special skills. Nonetheless, the number of scientists and engineers who are engaged in research and development activities has also grown rapidly. Between 1945 and 1955, the number of professional scientists in industrial laboratories rose to almost two and one-half times, while the number of supporting technicians doubled. This rise in research and development activities has both resulted from and led to many of the technological breakthroughs and scientific innovations in business and industry.

Table VI

Research Laboratories and Personnel in Eleven Selected Industries[1], 1945-55

	1945	1950	1955	Percent increase 1945–55
Number of laboratories	1,855	2,414	3,760	100
Scientists and engineers	50,560	70,182	119,641	140
Supporting personnel	70,544	87,547	141,256	100
Total laboratory personnel	121,104	157,729	260,897	114

1 These industries employ approximately 85 percent of all research people reported in the Directories of the National Research Council, Washington, D. C.

SOURCE: George Perazich, *Growth of Scientific Research in Selected Industries, 1945-1960,* a report prepared for the National Science Foundation, Washington, D. C., October 1957.

As employment of scientists and engineers by industry, government, and educational institutions has increased, expenditures for research and development projects have also been rising steadily. Although data for earlier years are not as accurate as more recent figures, it is reasonable to estimate that industry more than doubled such activities between 1946 and 1953. Total expenditures for research and development for 1953 were estimated to have exceeded $5 billion, and at the average postwar rate of growth could well have reached $7 billion to $8 billion by 1957. In other words, approximately 2 percent of gross national product in the United States is currently being devoted to research and development activities.

More than half of all research and development expenditures in 1953 was financed by federal funds, although less than 20 percent of the actual work was done in federal departments and agencies. Most of the government's research and development activities were channeled through private organizations. Thus, roughly three-quarters of all research and development can generally be deducted as a legitimate However, almost 40 percent of such industrial research was financed by the federal government, while industry financed the remainder from its own resources.

Table VII

Research and Development Expenditures, 1953
(In millions of dollars)

Sources of funds	Users of Funds					
	Federal government	Industry	Universities	Research institutes	Total	Percent
Federal government	970	1,520	280	50	2,810	52
Industry	—	2,350	20	—	2,370	44
Universities	—	—	130	—	130	3
Research institutes	—	—	30	20	50	1
Total	970	3,870	460	70	5,370	
Percent	18	72	9	1		100

NOTE: Detail may not add to totals because of rounding. Percentages calculated on the basis of unrounded figures.

SOURCE: *Reviews of Data on Research & Development*, No. 1, National Science Foundation, Dec. 1956.

One factor which has contributed to industrial research has been the high corporate tax rates of the past decade and a half. Outlays on research and development can generally be deducted as a legitimate business expense. Thus, the more venturesome companies have been encouraged steadily to increase expenditures for such activities which are conducted at a net cost to the company of much less than the actual amounts spent.

The high rates of expenditures on research and development by American industry are evidence of a growing recognition that it is necessary continuously to increase productivity in a dynamic and competitive economy like that of the United States. Technological advances permit rising output per man-hour and corresponding wage increases. Conversely, relatively high wages stimulate the adoption of more labor-saving techniques. Usually, in countries with relatively abundant labor and low wages, there is no strong incentive for the adoption of labor-saving techniques. In some cases, however, other reasons may justify the adoption of new technology by these countries. Improved methods and new discoveries often result in a better product than one produced by old methods. For example, a new automatic petroleum refinery can produce gasoline which has far greater uniformity than any obtained by the older method of repeatedly examining samples in a laboratory and then adjusting the mixture on the basis of these tests. Thus, many technological innovations introduced in the United States because of relatively high wage costs have also been adopted in countries with substantially lower wage costs because of the improvement in the quality of the product.

Nevertheless, technological advance does not necessarily lead to, nor has it always resulted in, unqualified human betterment. In the late eighteenth and nineteenth centuries, the new techniques which replaced handicrafts often deprived human labor of much of the dignity of work and the joy of creation. Increasingly in the twentieth century, however, self-regulating machines and automatic production processes have substantially reduced the time and energy which workers have had to devote to routine operations of hand and brain. Thus, one consequence of the gradual advance of mechanization—and, particularly, the more recent advance of automation—has been some restoration of the dignity and satisfaction of labor, though in forms different from those of pre-industrial societies. Today, the worker is no longer the slave of a machine but is becoming the supervisor and caretaker of production systems.

Modern research is at the heart of the dynamic economic process. It results in more and better products, often at lower prices despite rising costs. In the United States, the development, introduction, and absorption of the technological changes have helped to make possible the high productivity of the American worker. Many of these innovations are based on knowledge derived from other countries; many stem from and contribute to the mass production and mass market which are characteristic of the American economy. Regardless of their origin, scientific and technological advances will most certainly continue to make important contributions to a high rate of productivity in the American economy. The extent of these contributions will be governed not alone by the availability of a growing number of well-trained scientists and skilled technicians. It will be equally important that an adequate allocation of funds and resources be provided for the development of both fundamental and applied scientific knowledge. Urgent, too, is the reappraisal and improvement of the objectives, content, and methods of the American educational system.

Chapter VI

Capital

LABOR SKILLS, managerial competence, and technological advances can have their full effect on productivity and production only if sufficient capital is available to finance the required plant and equipment. A relatively abundant supply of capital results in greater productivity, which in turn generates even larger supplies of capital for further gains in productivity. Hence, an adequate stock of capital is an essential element in economic growth and, conversely, a scarcity of capital is a serious obstacle for countries seeking to hasten their economic development. For countries in the latter category, there is always a difficult choice of how to divide their limited resources between an inadequate consumption and an inadequate capital formation.

The Role of Foreign Capital

In the early stages of its industrialization, the United States—as in the case of other underdeveloped countries—had to meet its capital requirements not only by diverting domestic resources from consumption to investment, but also by attracting funds from abroad. Capital formation out of domestic resources was, as in most countries, larger and more dependable than the imported capital. But the import of foreign capital, principally private capital, was significant in American development until World War I. In 1914, private foreign investment in the United States amounted to over $7 billion, which in terms of purchasing power would be worth about $35 billion in current prices (see Appendix Table 12). Moreover, the $7 billion figure underestimates the actual role of foreign investment in American economic development before World War I, as some capital had already been repatriated by then. Nor does the figure include investments which were partial or complete financial losses for the investors although they did result in the creation of productive plant and equipment—for example, many railroads which went into bankruptcy after they were constructed but continued in operation.

Since 1914, private foreign investment in the United States has been a much less significant factor in American economic growth. The alternative of investment or consumption has also become a problem of diminishing importance. Today, gross national product and per capita income are large enough for the United States simultaneously to afford a rising standard of living and to provide a continuously growing and modernized stock of producers goods in industry, agriculture, and distribution. Indeed, total output is great enough to permit a high level of defense and foreign aid expenditures without serious interference with either domestic investment or consumption.

The Sources of Domestic Capital

In recent decades, the total amount of savings in the United States has been adequate not only to meet the needs of an expanding domestic economy but also to provide export capital for other countries. Only when there was a need for large-scale government borrowing during wars and at the peak of the investment boom of recent years did some scarcity of capital arise. However, capital abundance for some purposes and capital scarcity for other purposes may exist side by side. For an examination of the capital market in detail, it is necessary to take a look at various types of saving and investment.

The financial resources devoted to capital formation in the United States are savings of various kinds—individual, institutional, corporate, and governmental. In the early period of American development, the great bulk of productive investment was financed by the savings of wealthy individuals and families. While individual saving is still very important, the other types of saving have been growing more rapidly in recent decades and now contribute well over half of the total.

A comparison of the sources of private saving in the late 1920's and early 1950's shows important shifts. The shifts in the forms of individual saving have been especially marked. Additions to currency and deposit holdings of individuals have just about tripled as a percent of total private saving and have become an important source of funds for capital formation. Also, payments by individual consumers on installment credit, home mortgages, etc., have increased substantially. Formerly, the accumulation of the necessary savings preceded the purchase of an expensive automobile or item of household equipment or clothing. Today, the purchase often comes first and is followed by the necessary accumulation of savings to meet the payments under the installment contract. In contrast, individual saving in the form of the private acquisition of securities has declined drastically—from around 47 percent of total private saving to only 11 percent.

Spectacular increases have occurred in recent decades in the invest-

Table VIII

Private National Saving by Major Components
(Annual averages)

Net additions to:	1926–29 $ billion	1926–29 Percent	1953–56 $ billion	1953–56 Percent
Individual saving	5.7	58.7	13.5	44.7
Currency and deposits	1.0	10.3	9.1	30.1
Private securities (stocks and bonds)	4.6	47.4	3.4	11.3
Other net saving[1]	.1	1.0	1.0	3.3
Institutional saving	1.7	17.6	8.5	28.1
Private insurance and pension reserves	1.5	15.5	5.3	17.5
Government insurance and pension reserves	.2	2.1	3.2	10.6
Corporate saving[2]	2.3	23.7	8.2	27.2
Total private saving	9.7	100.0	30.2	100.0

[1] Includes additions to individual holdings of government securities and all durable goods assets, less additions to liabilities (e.g. installment credit obligations, mortgages, etc.).
[2] Retained profits.

SOURCES: 1926-29—Raymond W. Goldsmith, *A Study of Saving in the United States*, Princeton University Press, Princeton, 1955, Volume 1, Tables S-5 and S-35; 1953-56—*Survey of Current Business*, July 1957.

ment funds of private and public institutional programs. These consist of insurance and welfare funds of private business enterprises and of trade unions and other nonprofit organizations, as well as government insurance and pension programs. Such institutional savings not only make possible accident, sickness, retirement, death, and other substantial benefits for the great majority of American families, but also contribute a large portion of the funds needed for new capital formation each year. Through these institutions, individual American workers and middle-income groups contribute indirectly to the capital supply of the country. At the end of 1957, for example, private pension plans alone were believed to hold approximately $34 billion of invested assets—about three-quarters in the form of corporate bonds and stocks—and to be growing at a rate which was more than $3.5 billion per year. In this way, millions of American workers have been receiving indirectly the benefits of securities ownership—dividends and appreciation of stock values. Trade unions have in a number of instances also become large-scale investors in corporate stocks and various kinds of business enterprises.

The savings of business corporations constitute the third major source of funds for capital formation. The relative importance of corporate savings as a percent of total private saving has remained about the same throughout the period. This source of savings is particularly important for business investment and capital expansion, and its significance is demonstrated by the ratio of gross corporate savings—that is, depreciation and retained profits—to capital investment. In 1956, for instance, gross corporate savings amounted to $42 billion, while business investments (excluding changes in inventories) were $61 billion. Thus, over 60 percent of industrial expansion and modernization is financed by these internal funds.

Table IX

Uses and Sources of Funds by Corporations and Financial Institutions (Annual averages)

	1922–29		1953–56	
	$ billion	Percent	$ billion	Percent
Uses				
Plant and equipment	7.5	61.5	25.1	74.0
Change in investments	.7	5.7	3.1	9.2
Change in other assets	4.0	32.8	5.7	16.8
Total uses	12.2	100.0	33.9	100.0
Sources				
Retained profits	2.5	20.5	7.2[1]	21.2
Depreciation	4.6[2]	37.7	14.3	42.2
Net new issues	3.0[3]	24.6	7.1	21.0
Change in other liabilities	3.8	31.1	5.6	16.5
Total sources	13.9	113.9	34.2	100.9
Statistical discrepancy	−1.7	−13.9	−.3	−.9

[1]Includes depletion.
[2]Includes other capital consumption allowances, such as depletion.
[3]Includes only net proceeds from sales of securities to noncorporate domestic buyers.
Sources: 1922-29—Raymond W. Goldsmith, *op.cit.*, Vol. II, Table B-19; 1953-56—"Financing Corporate Expansion in 1956," *Survey of Current Business*, September 1957.

Such self-financing has both advantages and disadvantages. On the one hand, there are substantial benefits which flow from relative freedom of action by aggressive and imaginative business managers. The rate of new development and technological innovation probably would be smaller if business management had to subject every new investment to the cautious scrutiny of the capital markets and the lending institutions. On the other hand, some waste undoubtedly results from this independence of the outside discipline of the capital market. Also, many small and medium-sized businesses are not able to satisfy more than a minor percentage of their new capital needs out of their own corporate savings. Despite this disadvantage, however, the magnitude of corporate self-financing has been important in making possible the high rate of productivity growth and expansion in the American economy.

The Use of Capital

Personal saving in recent years has been high in the United States. At the same time, however, savings use has also been high. In 1956, for example, consumer debt—both for installment and noninstallment credit purchases—increased by $3 billion. Also, consumers invested an additional $11 billion in residential mortgage debt. On balance, consumers provided $20 billion of net savings for financing business investment (including residential construction) and for borrowing by federal, state, and local governments for schools, roads, and other public works (see Appendix Table 13). Nevertheless, in view of the rates of savings use and of capital investment, the competition for available capital funds might well have reduced the rate of growth of the American economy had industry not been able to finance the major portion of its expansion and modernization from its own savings.

However, the fact that a large portion of total savings is absorbed by consumer installment buying and residential construction does not mean that this part of savings makes no contribution to increases in productivity. Without availability of funds for consumer credit, especially installment credit, there would be no mass market for consumer durable goods. Also, without ample mortgage credit at reasonable terms, 5.7 million privately financed new houses would not have been constructed during the past five years—which, in turn, created a mass market for building materials and home furnishings. Only the existence of a mass market makes adoption of many technological advances feasible.

The early financial development of American industry was not unlike that of many less developed countries today—the fact that both domestic and foreign sources of investment funds were forthcoming made possible a steady increase in capital formation. Within recent decades, the accumulation of savings by large groups of individuals and institutions has become an important source of investment capital and has made more widespread the gains from economic growth and development. It seems clear that the relatively high liquidity of the American economy—in itself a result of high productivity—has in turn contributed to advances in productivity, and will make further advances possible.

Chapter VII

Government

THERE IS general agreement that natural resources, labor and managerial skills, the drive for technological innovation, and the relative abundance of capital are indispensable in making possible the high productivity of the American economy. But opinion is far from unanimous with respect to the proper role and relative importance of another factor—the policies and actions of government. There are those who cling to the nineteenth-century view of government. They believe that the government's contribution to productivity should be limited to maintaining law and order and to providing only essential public services in the fields of education, health, highways, and sanitation. At the other extreme are the views of those who advocate various degrees of government control or even government ownership of the means of production.

The function of government in the United States corresponds to neither of these extremes. The American economy is predominantly organized by private enterprise, yet the government does not play only the night watchman's role. Experience has proved that vigorous and responsible private enterprise on the one hand, with constructive and prudent government policy on the other, are compatible. Under this system, high and rising productivity and living standards have been achieved without centralized authoritarian control of the economic process. The attainment of economic welfare has been fully consistent with the preservation of America's essential democratic freedoms. This effective reconciliation of potentially conflicting values has been accomplished by ensuring that the activities of government supplement and complement, but do not supersede, the activities of private entrepreneurs and consumers.

In the United States, governmental activities affect the economic process in widely different ways. Some of these governmental policies and programs are designed to assist and protect private initiative and enterprise in agriculture, industry, commerce, transportation, and finance. Others consist of enforcing a multitude of regulations and restrictions designed to protect the rights or the well-being of labor and consumers generally and of such relatively weak or underprivileged groups as small farmers, the unemployed, the handicapped, and the aged. Many of these governmental activities are long-standing; they have continued in most instances from one political administration to another.

Development of Natural Resources

Throughout the history of the United States, the government has been active in the development of agricultural and other natural resources. The federal government's public land policy was a major factor in the expansion of American agriculture. In 1862, the Homestead Act provided millions of farms of 160 acres each free to anyone living on them for five years. In the same year, the Morrill Act granted free land for the establishment of colleges and agricultural experiment stations throughout the nation. As we have noted, these training, research, and information facilities, supported or subsidized by the government, have contributed importantly to increases in agricultural productivity. In addition, they laid the groundwork for the establishment and development of the U.S. Department of Agriculture's Extension Service, which assists farmers in adopting advances in farm technology. A more controversial series of governmental programs dealing with agricultural price supports, production controls, and surplus commodities began in the interwar years. These varied farm programs have been designed to correct a lack of balance in supply and demand arising from world economic changes, technological advances, and depressions and wars. Sharp differences of opinion about the success or failure of these policies in achieving a better balance of supply and demand, and about their effects on farm prices and income, have continued to the present. To some extent, policies designed to reduce surplus production through curtailment of acreage have unintentionally induced farmers to grow more on their remaining land, and thereby have contributed to technological progress and the increase in farm productivity.

The conservation and development of other natural resources also have been an important concern of government, and have been promoted in a variety of ways. In the field of conservation, governmental policies and programs have been responsible for the preservation and renewal of valuable national forest resources and for the expansion, protection, and purification of water supplies needed for human, agricultural, and industrial consumption and for recreation.

As one aspect of its multipurpose water programs, the government has developed hydroelectric power to an extent that more than half of all hydroelectric power generated in the United States is now publicly owned. Similarly, the government is active not only in the development of nuclear power, but also in the research related to solar energy, extraction of oil from shale, and the hydrogenation of coal. Substantial tax concessions given to petroleum producers are the equivalent of an incentive subsidy to stimulate the output of this essential fuel and chemical raw material. The production of various metals—copper, silver, uranium, etc.—is also stimulated by governmental action through tax concessions, bounties, tariff protection, purchases for the strategic stockpile, and in other ways.

Stimulus to Industry

Governmental aid in the development and operation of various forms of transportation not only has directly benefited productivity but also has stimulated the production of many natural resources. Before the coming of the railroads, inland transportation depended upon roads and canals, most of which were constructed with the help of federal and state grants, subsidies, or tax concessions. Many of the railroads had similar help. From 1850 to 1871 alone, about 183 million acres of federal and state lands were given free to the railroad companies, thereby making possible the construction of the present main railroad network of the United States. Development of the relatively new truck and bus transportation industries has been greatly facilitated by the construction and maintenance of more than three million miles of highways and roadways by federal, state, and local governments.

Since 1845, the maritime shipping industry has had special governmental subsidies for carrying mail. More recently, certain tax advantages and subsidies for ship construction have been available to private operators. In addition, the legislation requiring, as a rule, that 50 percent of foreign-aid cargoes must be shipped in American vessels has constituted another indirect subsidy to private shipping companies. The commercial air transport industry, too, has received governmental assistance in the forms of mail subsidies, aircraft development contracts, and public maintenance and operation of ground facilities and air traffic control systems.

Governmental policies and programs contribute importantly to the productivity of the labor force. In addition to the indispensable contributions to the health and education of the working force are various social welfare programs which help to maintain the efficiency of workers. Morale is fostered by the government's guarantee of the rights of labor to organize trade unions of their own choosing and to bargain collectively. Whereas collective bargaining is solely the function of management and labor in the United States, the government, when requested, provides mediation, conciliation, and arbitration services.

Government's many services to management and business enterprise contribute directly or indirectly to the productivity of the American economy. Important among these are many statistical and informational services. Such guides not only help management to forecast long-range economic trends but are also needed for day-to-day operations and training, research, and development activities. Though there are still some important gaps in the data needed for appraising economic conditions and prospects—more adequate data on savings and consumer expenditures, for example—this free flow of information from government agencies is vital to the successful operation of the American business system. Other examples are governmental assistance to business—such as that provided by the Bureau of Standards—in establishing standards of performance or quality for many new and existing products. And on another front, in addition to its well-established, active role in promoting international trade relations and in fostering export markets, the government's participation at international trade fairs has encouraged private American businesses to seek foreign customers.

Particularly during the past two decades, the government's direct and indirect support of scientific research and technological development has been a major spur to American productivity. Much of the new technology which is making possible the so-called "second industrial revolution" has been a by-product of the government's defense interest in such fields as electronics, synthetics and new materials, automatic computers and control devices, and nuclear energy. However, the government has also conducted or financed many research programs of a nonmilitary nature which, by discovering new or more efficient uses of abundant natural resources, have produced important reactions in major industries. Even when research is undertaken solely on the initiative of private industry, the government's stimulus is present in the form of favorable tax provisions.

Enlargement of the Supply of Capital

Governmental policies and programs also foster the supply of capital. The government first began extending credit through the creation of facilities for farm credit, but during the depression years of the 1930's government credit was made available to virtually all kinds of business.

The housing finance program, started during the 1930's, has become a permanent government activity. It is an outstanding example of the dovetailing of government policy and private enterprise. Houses are built by private contractors and most are financed by private mortgages. The government, however, has had a decisive influence on the terms of the mortgages, the type of houses built through the insurance and guarantee programs, and the establishment of standards for houses financed in this manner. The Federal Housing Administration and the Veterans Administration support private construction by granting guarantees and insurance for a small fee, and about half of all nonfarm housing construction is financed by private loans covered by such government guarantees or insurance. The Farm Credit Administration and the Farmers Home Administration provide loans for farm ownership and improvement, for farm housing and other farm buildings, and for farm operation.

The importance of total government loan programs can be measured by the fact that on June 30, 1957, outstanding direct federal loans amounted to $17.5 billion, or about 4 percent of the total private debt of all kinds. Loans insured or guaranteed by the government totaled another $56 billion, or an additional 13 percent of the total private debt. Further strength is given to the credit structure by the operations of such government agencies as the Federal Deposit Insurance Corporation, which insures each bank deposit account up to $10,000.

Another federal activity which began during the depression is the social insurance program. In 1956, 68 million workers were covered under the Old-Age and Survivors Insurance program; and approximately 38 million were eligible for unemployment insurance benefits which the federal government provides in cooperation with the states.

Promotion of Full Employment and Economic Growth

Under the Employment Act of 1946, the government was made responsible for a policy designed to promote "maximum employment, production and purchasing power." While the government all through American history has promoted certain sectors of the economy, a policy related to general economic growth and stability introduced a new element of responsibility. This policy does not require, however, any interference with the decisions of business, labor, or consumers —it is to be conducted as far as possible through general fiscal and monetary measures and other programs within the existing authority of the government.

The general role of government in the American economy can best be demonstrated by what has been called the national economic account or the nation's economic budget. This shows a rise—expressed in current dollars—in federal, state, and local government transactions from less than 10 percent of total production (gross national product) in 1929 to 25 percent in 1956. This 25 percent figure includes all government purchases of goods and wages for government employees, as well as the so-called "transfer payments" to farmers, social security recipients, veterans, and bondholders. Transactions supported by government guarantees or insurance—Federal Housing Administration mortgages, for example—are reflected in the private sector of the economy. To that extent, the economic budget understates the influence of the government on the economy.

Table X

The Nation's Economic Budget, 1929 and 1956
(Percent distribution by major sectors)

Economic groups	1929 Receipts	1929 Expenditures	1956 Receipts	1956 Expenditures
Consumers (disposable income and consumption expenditures)	79.6	75.7	69.2	64.4
Business (retained earnings and domestic investment)	11.0	15.5	9.9	15.9
Net foreign investment	—	.7	—	.3
Government (including transfers, interest, and subsidies)	10.7	9.7	26.3	25.1
Less: Transfers, interest and subsidies	1.6	1.6	5.8	5.8
Government (net receipts and purchases of goods and services)	9.1	8.1	20.5	19.4
Statistical discrepancy	+.3		+.4	
Gross national product	100.0	100.0	100.0	100.0

SOURCE: For figures in current dollars, see Appendix Table 13.

Attitudes Toward Governmental Action

Because the American economic system is dynamic and because the relationships among major functional groups are constantly changing, the government may be doing too much or too little at any given time—and often it may be guilty of both in different economic areas. Thus, there are always greater or lesser disagreements and controversies over the specific policies and programs of the government. But, such differences of interest and opinion are the essence of democracy.

It is significant that such disagreements are rarely irreconcilable and controversies do not extend to basic economic institutions. For example, no important political party or functional group in the United States has ever advocated the nationalization of industry. In fact, businessmen and workers have been equally opposed to nationalization. Both recognize that, in addition to the substantial loss of individual freedom that would result, the economic well-being of each group is better served when each remains free to bargain with the other over wages, hours, and working conditions under general rules and regulations established by the government.

The United States is far from having achieved a perfect blending of free enterprise and governmental responsibilities in the economic sphere. There are some who believe that the government at times has been subservient to powerful economic interests and its policies and programs appeared to be designed to benefit the privileged few. Others believe that at times the government has played so preponderant a role that the freedom and vitality of private enterprise were seriously jeopardized. The United States now seems to be approaching a situation in which neither business, labor, farmers, nor government has disproportionate influence. Each sector is vigorous, dynamic, and powerful, but each recognizes that it will be curbed if its actions adversely affect the general welfare. One important result of this development has been greater mutual confidence among all of these groups; and the consequent improvement in the morale of business managers, workers, farmers, professional people, and government administrators has contributed importantly to the growth of American productivity.

These highlights of the various aspects of the government's contributions to the growth of productivity in the American economy demonstrate that the United States does not have a laissez-faire economy, even though the great bulk of its economic transactions occur as the result of private initiative and choice. The government's responsibility—which has gradually evolved, largely through trial and error—is to provide those resources, services, stimuli, and regulations without which a private enterprise economy could not function either in the general interest or with high efficiency. Indeed, the examples given permit a conclusion of major significance, not only for the United States but also for other countries. This is that active and intelligent participation by government in certain phases of the economic process is not only compatible with a basically private enterprise economy but, in the conditions of the mid-twentieth century, it may be indispensable to the effective functioning of private enterprise systems.

Chapter VIII

Values and Institutions

OUR ACCOUNT of the principal factors responsible for high American productivity still does not explain why the American economy differs, except in degree, from the economies of the other Western democracies. That it differs cannot be denied. Many visitors from other countries have said they were unprepared for a number of distinctive features of the American system—its dynamism, its competitiveness, its relatively equitable income distribution, its flexibility and resourcefulness.

The American economy is an intrinsic part of the wider system of relationships and meanings comprising American society as a whole. The interrelationships between economic and noneconomic factors are complex. However, even an admittedly simplified and impressionistic description can indicate those American attitudes and institutions which determine the spirit in which American economic activities are conducted. These values are among the most important factors to be included in an explanation of the high productivity of the American economy.

A New Beginning in America

Historically, one basic American attitude has been what Reinhold Niebuhr has called the expectation of "a new beginning." Goethe expressed this thought 130 years ago when he wrote:

> America, you have it better
> Than our continent, the old.
> You have no ruined castles
> Nor broken basalt columns.
> You can live in the present
> Without being restrained
> By frustrating conflicts
> Or futile recollections
> Of the past.

Goethe referred not only to the obvious fact that, when the first European colonists came to these shores, America was a virgin land

and settlers did not have to fit into any pre-existing traditions and institutions. He also meant that each successive wave of settlers could leave behind those aspects of their native cultures which they found most frustrating.

In another context, President Franklin D. Roosevelt once made the classic remark that Americans "are all immigrants or descendants of immigrants." Some came to America against their wills—the slaves and the indentured servants of the colonial period. But the great majority of the newcomers, from the first settlement until the present, have migrated voluntarily. These were resolved to leave behind in the "old country" the traditions which had become meaningless and to develop or adopt new attitudes, customs, and institutions. To them, America offered a new opportunity for the fulfillment of hopes and aspirations.

For some, the new beginning was mainly religious or political; to others, the new beginning was primarily social and economic. For most people, there were differing combinations of these—and other—motives. The desire to escape religious persecution meant that effective freedom of worship would eventually prevail in the new settlements. The desire for self-government led to the establishment in the American colonies of institutions of local, and of representative, government. Finally, the desire for economic independence and improved social positions gave rise to individual aspirations which would not be limited by inherited social and family status or legal and economic disabilities.

Thus, the predominant expectation of most migrants to these shores over the past 350 years has been to create or find here a new society in which the self-reliant and responsible individual could live his own life free of the limitations of traditionalist communities, with their preordained and fixed hierarchies. True, there were numerous attempts to establish or maintain religious uniformity, centralized oligarchical government, feudalistic land tenures, and mercantilistic commercial and industrial restrictions. But eventually, religious diversity and equality, universal suffrage and decentralized local government, freedom of enterprise and a high degree of social mobility were triumphant.

The Early American Environment

This distinctive development was also nurtured by the frontier, which provided a physical means for a new beginning. Any attempt to enforce religious uniformity, authoritarian government, or unduly restrictive economic arrangements would encourage those dissatisfied and unable to resist successfully to move on and make another new beginning on the continuously advancing frontier. In fact, this situation in many cases effectively discouraged such restrictive attempts.

In one sense, the term "frontier" has had a broader connotation for Americans than the geographical belts of territory beyond the edge of established farms and towns. Even in the settled portions of the country, there were always new directions and activities into which economic enterprise could be extended. It is in this sense that the frontier still exists, and is still accessible to initiative and courage. Temperament and experience still determine the particular frontier on which a man can seek his new beginning.

The geographical frontier of the past, however, significantly influenced the development of certain typically American characteristics. The way of life required on newly settled lands encouraged certain traits and social attitudes which have helped to shape the image of "the good society" in America. On the one hand, coping successfully with the dangers, hardships, and difficulties of frontier life placed a premium upon individual self-reliance, resourcefuless, practicality, and versatility. On the other hand, a high degree of mutual help and social cooperation was required to accomplish necessary tasks which were beyond the strength of the single individual or family—clearing the land, building homes and transportation facilities, and protecting the community against human and natural enemies. Moreover, the establishment of rudimentary local goverment institutions and the maintenance of law and order were usually the responsibility of the settlers themselves—a situation which fostered decentralized decision making and a democratic political life.

But the frontier environment was not the only major influence in the evolution of these characteristic traits and social attitudes. Important, too, were the distinctive "ideologies" of New England and Virginia. The Puritanism of the former was largely a product of what Max Weber has called "the Protestant ethic and the spirit of capitalism." Hard work, frugality, and thrift—and the economic success which frequently attended the practice of these virtues—contributed to a man's conviction that he was one of the few chosen for salvation. Though the theological aspects of this ideology declined by the late eighteenth century, the basic attitude persisted in the form of New England "Yankeeism," with its characteristic self-reliance, conscientiousness, competitive shrewdness, and entrepreneurial vigor.

Virginia's contribution was the adaptation of the doctrines of the European Enlightenment to the American environment. As expressed in the thinking and writings of such Virginians as Thomas Jefferson and James Madison, these views emphasized the power of human reason, the possibilities of social progress and improvement, and the natural rights of the individual to life, liberty, and the pursuit of happiness. However, the Virginia philosophers never succumbed to Rousseau's illusions about the goodness of human nature and the perfectibility of man, and they were closer to Hobbes and Locke in warning against the destructive potential of human passions and the need to balance individual liberty and personal equality with political power and social order. It was in the succeeding generations of the nineteenth century that the exuberance and success of American society fostered widespread convictions about the omnipotence of human reason and the inevitability of individual and social perfection. These beliefs became important ingredients in the essentially optimistic and rationalistic American character today.

Other significant influences also helped to shape American society. One was the large measure of mutual toleration necessary to permit people from so many different cultural, religious, and racial backgrounds to cooperate successfully in building an essentially democratic society. Important, too, has been the effect of the sheer physical size and relative self-sufficiency of the United States in making possible the largest free trade area in the world. These and many other factors supplemented and reinforced one another in giving to American society its distinctive characteristics.

The Effects of Indigenous American Characteristics

Thus, American society since its beginning has been characterized in greater or lesser degree by such attitudes as an orientation toward the present and future and not toward the past; a predisposition to base thought and action on the facts of the existing situation rather than upon inherited custom or abstract doctrine; a deep confidence in the power of rational thought and human action to solve personal and social problems; and a willingness to compromise or accommodate competing group and individual interests. By and large, American society has been optimistic, pragmatic, rationalistic, open-minded, and cooperative. It has tended to value conscientious work, material well-being, technical skill, individual flexibility, and social and geographical mobility. These values have contributed to American economic success and in turn have been strengthened by it.

These characteristics have not been unmixed benefits. While they have enabled the American people to solve or avoid many problems which perplex other countries, they have created difficulties and disadvantages of their own. For example, the absence of a strong sense of the past has saved American society from the bondage of outworn concepts and obsolete techniques. At the same time, however, it has denied to many Americans the sustaining consciousness of belonging to a long, unbroken historical tradition. Again, a faith in the power of human reason and the inevitability of social progress has motivated American science and technology and helped to make possible the substantial justice and welfare achieved in American society. Yet, this faith at times has led to complacency which took for granted American superiority in science and technology. It has also impeded the understanding of domestic and international political and economic realities, and is largely responsible for the naiveté and moralism which have sometimes characterized certain of our actions at home and abroad. Finally, the willingness of individuals and groups to cooperate and to participate constructively in community life has held American society together despite the heterogeneous cultural and racial origins of its people and their multiplicity of particular loyalties and interests. But this essential benefit has been bought at the cost of considerable pressure on individuals to conform to socially accepted patterns of life.

These American attitudes, intangible and ambivalent as they are, have been major shaping influences on business and farm management, on labor's dedication to work, and on government policies. With some exaggeration, we may say that in most other industrial countries the first choice of management is to continue the organization and technique of production used in the past and to change only if the gain is substantial and beyond doubt. American management has a propensity to change and is much less likely to cling to familiar organizations and techniques. Workers and farmers, too, in America are more willing to accept new techniques and to undergo necessary adjustments than is usual in other countries. Finally, the absence of dogmatism and the strength of a pragmatic spirit have permitted the government to adopt policies which appeared in the interest of economic growth and to change or drop such policies when they are no longer needed.

A recent report summarizing the impressions of one of the productivity teams which have come to America from other countries probably expressed the opinions of many foreign observers: "Before coming to America we thought the only reason for high productivity in America was machines and gadgets. Now we find that efficiency and high output per man-hour is a way of thinking on the part of management, engineers, technicians, and labor; a way of thinking which induces each to exert his best for the welfare of all."

There have been few—if any—periods in the history of civilization when the conditions of life have changed as rapidly or as drastically as in the twentieth century. The scientific and technological "explosion," the revolution of rising expectations in virtually all countries, the contemporary ideological conflicts, and the unparalleled destructive potential of modern warfare—all have combined to force even democratic governments to assume a greater and greater degree of centralized power. Yet, thanks to its basic values and institutions, the American political and economic system has adapted to the requirements of these changing conditions without fundamentally impairing the decentralized and private character of its decision making and activities. True, the changing conditions of life in the twentieth century have affected the kind and extent of the possible choices now available to Americans. But—whether as a producer, investor, or consumer—the individual American still has wide freedom in determining his fate.

Social, cultural, political, and religious factors indigenous to the United States have shaped the development and use of economic resources, the willingness to accept change and technological innovation, and the role of government in the economic process. They make up a large and essential part of what might be called "the spirit" which animates the economy of the American people. And it is this spirit which has enabled the American economy to preserve its distinctive dynamism, flexibility, and large measure of distributive justice despite the strongly centralizing and authoritarian pressures of our times. Beyond the more tangible economic factors discussed in the preceding chapters, the characteristic values and institutions of American society have been crucial factors in creating the high productivity of the American economy. Their persistence inspires our confidence that a rise in productivity will continue over the coming years and that the economic and social problems of the next decade will be tackled in a creative and democratic fashion.

Part Two

Problems and Prospects of the American Economy

The American economy presents a picture in which most producers —workers as well as managers—are bent on creative accomplishments through use of the latest advances in technology and in the art of management. While this is a picture of which Americans have reason to be proud, it is not without flaws. In this part of our report, we point out some of these sources of dissatisfaction and indicate policy measures that have been proposed for dealing with them.

Marxist opponents of the American system have always insisted that its deficiencies, far from being correctable, will inevitably produce recurrent and ever more severe crises. Other critics, while not sharing that conviction of doom, doubt the possibility of progress under a predominantly free enterprise system and claim that recent achievements in the American economy have arisen from exceptional circumstances not likely to continue. These notions have resulted partly from a failure to understand the strength of the capacity for self-criticism and social reform inherent in American society.

The recurring waves of reform in America's history have not been inspired by abstract doctrines, but by the desire to correct specific abuses and actual deficiencies believed to be incompatible with the democratic and individualistic ideals of American society. And the reforms have never stemmed solely from one source.

The social and economic accomplishments during these periods of reform resulted from ever-shifting alliances and combinations among different groups, sections, and political parties throughout the country. Both the Democratic and Republican parties, and their predecessors, traditionally have contained liberal and conservative wings. The more single-minded "third" parties were usually able to achieve portions of their programs only when they were allied with, or absorbed by, one of the two major parties. However, their existence was often the necessary stimulus to the advocacy of reform measures by the Democrats or Republicans.

Because of these varied supporters, most changes during reform periods have been compromises. On the one hand, Americans have widely held the conviction that justice demands an equal chance for personal fulfillment; that it is both possible and proper to improve the individual's situation and the conditions of society as a whole; and that the government has a responsibility to foster and assist the people's efforts to improve themselves. On the other hand, there has been the deeply rooted American concern for individual freedom; the belief that the government is the helpmate and not the master of the people; and the conviction that improvements must result primarily from the will and effort of the people themselves. In effect, the ability to achieve so many benefits without resort to highly centralized authoritarian institutions reflects this creative tension between social justice and individual freedom in American society.

The first major reform movement in America was during the period from 1800 to 1840. The early phase of this movement has been called "Jeffersonian democracy" and the later, more radical phase "Jacksonian democracy." Though there were differences between the two, their combined result was achievement of actual or potential equality of political power and of participation in the political process for all groups of Americans. Among the most important accomplishments were universal suffrage, popular election of legislators and judges, revision of state constitutions to increase popular control over state and local governments, and the beginnings of universal free education. The farmers and urban workers, who provided the popular support for Jeffersonian and Jacksonian democracy, also sought certain economic reforms. The farmers obtained more liberal policies for disposal of the western lands owned by the government, easy access to cheap credit, and low tariff and other governmental measures which would make the international and domestic terms of trade more favorable to agricultural producers. The workers, particularly those in the newly established factories of the Northeast, were increasingly successful in obtaining repeal of state and local legislation and reversal of judicial decisions which prohibited the formation of trade unions and the use of the strike.

By the late 1840's the rise of the slavery issue began to induce a regrouping of parties and platforms. The realignment that emerged during the next decade was itself a great reform effort, whose dramatic development during the ensuing Civil War and reconstruction period transformed the economic and social life of all sections of the country. These years were noteworthy not only for the abolition of slavery, but also for the determined, though abortive, efforts of the Reconstruction Republicans to enforce full and equal—almost exclusive in some areas—participation of Negroes in political and economic life. By 1875, manufacturing industry dominated the North, and free homesteads and new transcontinental railroads were rapidly filling the West with farmers, ranchers, and miners. In contrast, the South entered upon a long period of virtual economic stagnation from which it began slowly to recover only after the turn of the century. These developments re-emphasized old, and created new, problems which provided objectives for revived reform movements.

Broadly speaking, there were common characteristics and a cumulative process in the succession of reform efforts from the late 1870's to the end of the 1930's. The main impulse to organize these reform efforts in a political form came first from the western farmers, who were joined somewhat later by other discontented groups. The earlier Populist and Progressive parties, their counterparts in the liberal wings of the Democratic and Republican parties, and their more radical predecessors and offshoots—all expressed a similar basic concern to achieve greater social justice and economic welfare for those Americans who were, in the term current during the New Deal era of the 1930's, "underprivileged."

The definition of those who were underprivileged differed from section to section and from decade to decade. In the industrial North and Midwest, it was mainly the industrial workers—at first virtually all of them, but later primarily those in the mass production and other unorganized industries whose interests were not represented by the craft unions. In the agricultural West, it was the farmers, predominantly those operating family farms, who felt that they were not obtaining fair prices and incomes. In the South, the politically active, discontented group was at first the small white farmers; but in the 1930's the plight of southern Negroes began to cause increasing concern, not only outside the South but also within the southern states themselves. In the Mountain States, it was the important mining industry which sought help whenever the prices of nonferrous metals dropped too low. And it was the combined interests of businessmen, farmers, and consumers on the Pacific Coast who demanded that they be provided with adequate transportation and power facilities.

Reform groups usually sought two types of legislation. The first type would require the government to enforce certain rights of the underprivileged, or limit unfair or undesirable practices by more powerful groups. A notable example is the labor-management legislation of the 1930's, which not only validated the workers' right to organize and bargain collectively in trade unions of their own choosing but also established governmental machinery for enforcing this right. An example in the social field is the as yet only partially successful federal legislation which attempts to prohibit discrimination of all kinds against Negroes and other racial and religious minorities. The regulation of railroad rates and practices, and antitrust legislation are still others.

The second kind of legislation usually was aimed at governmental programs for increasing the substandard incomes or welfare of groups with a precarious economic status or naturally weak economic bargaining power. Examples in this category include wage and hour legislation; old-age and survivors' insurance; federal aid for slum clearance and housing for low-income groups; and many other forms of federal, state, and local expenditures designed to improve the economic position of particular groups.

This continuing self-criticism and the resulting reforms in American society strikingly refute the Marxist contentions that the "misery of the masses" will increase under a free enterprise system and that the government is only "the executive committee of the ruling class." The political and economic power of the captains of industry and large corporations was never as great as Marxist theory assumed. Not only did popular reform movements rooted in agricultural and labor groups serve to check it, but only a generation or two was needed for industrialists to develop to the point where they themselves began to participate in the task of correcting the institutional deficiencies of the American system.

There were always individuals and small, though articulate, groups who opposed every step of reform to the bitter end. Also, there were often serious controversies over specific objectives and methods of reform. These differences could only slow down and moderate, but not prevent, changes that were widely believed necessary and desirable. Nor was there any major group in American society which was completely and fundamentally opposed to change and improvement. Power was sufficiently dispersed among the major social groups to enable all, sooner or later, to share in the increasing justice and welfare.

The major test of this acceptance of change and of the capacity for practical reform of all major groups in American society came during the depression of the 1930's. Businessmen were paralyzed by dwindling sales and vanishing assets; farmers were losing their farms and their markets; workers were faced with seemingly endless unemployment; dispossessed home owners and savers helplessly watched as bank deposits and insurance policies were wiped out—all of these shocking developments created a sense of despair, frustration, and anger. For a time, the federal and state governments seemed unable to do anything except plead futilely for a return of confidence, and unintentionally reduce effective demand still further by curtailing expenditures and increasing taxes. In consequence, some observers confidently predicted that the United States would soon follow the totalitarian examples of Fascist Italy, Nazi Germany, or Communist Russia. But only a negligible fraction of Americans toyed with these revolutionary proposals of the left or right.

Desperate and fearful though they were, most Americans were far more interested in immediate measures to correct specific problems than in a fundamental reorganization of the entire economic and social system. Thus, the farmers wanted an agricultural price support program and protection against mortgage foreclosures; the workers pressed for employment-creating public works expenditures and unemployment insurance and relief; home owners were interested in mortgage guarantees, and savers in federal insurance of bank deposits and supervision of the securities markets; and so on.

It is true that inadequate understanding of the nature of economic depressions and the persistence of obsolete remedies and prejudices prevented the adoption of sufficiently effective recovery measures, and large-scale unemployment consequently persisted until the end of the 1930's. But, though complete recovery was delayed, the years of the New Deal witnessed the culmination and fruition of many of the social and economic reform movements of the post-Civil War period.

Under the impact of the depression of the 1930's, the need for positive reform measures was so widely recognized and the resistance to them so weakened that previously impossible changes were accomplished with comparative rapidity. Furthermore, many of these reform measures could not have been carried out had it not been for the substantial economic growth of the 1940's and 1950's. Resumption of economic growth from the depth of the depression permitted far greater increases in incomes than could have been obtained through redistribution of a static national income. The rise in incomes also enabled the United States to avoid paralyzingly bitter domestic controversies and conflicts over division of the national product.

The American economy, then, has been in a process of rapid evolution—at times so rapid that some of the problems soon became meaningless and were superseded by the different problems of a subsequent period. Whereas certain of the policy measures adopted—some of those, for example, instituted in periods of depression and war—were only temporary, others have had a lasting impact on the American economy.

Nor has change come to an end. New problems are on the economic and social horizons and policies will have to be devised to deal with them. We do not claim that we know how to overcome all the existing and foreseeable shortcomings. It is the challenge of the age that many of the old concepts and answers do not fit these emerging problems, and new approaches are needed.

Important for the solution of these problems is the gradual development of an image of what a desirable social and economic life would be in the future. Simply saying that abundance is the economic goal would be too vague. Lifting all incomes significantly above the minimum needed for existence is a more specific and immediate objective. Giving everyone sufficient leisure and a broad enough education to participate constructively in the cultural life of the country is another goal within our reach.

These are aspirations found everywhere. But in addition, there is another American goal which has been expressed more often and more strongly here than in other parts of the world. This is that all Americans should own enough property to give them a feeling of economic security and personal independence. This objective has been sought from the earliest days of American history. A major expression of it was the Homestead Act of 1862, whose underlying philosophy was that every American who wished should possess property adequate for his family's needs. That there has been in the United States this ideal of economic security through individual property ownership was perhaps one of the reasons why the drive for governmental social security measures developed here so much later than in Europe. Today, most Americans believe both that government social security programs are important and should be adequate to take care of emergency and subsistence needs, and that broadening the distribution of private property remains a highly desirable continuing objective.

In the following chapters, we will deal both with problems of the future and with those of more immediate significance. Among the latter, we need to improve our ability to maintain reasonably full employment and a fair degree of price stability; prevent monopoly; adjust education, research, and training to the requirements of modern technology and international problems; promote the international flow of capital, goods, and knowledge; conserve natural resources and develop substitutes for energy and raw materials needed by a growing world population.

We believe that these tasks can and will be carried out within the framework of a free and democratic society. We see no signs indicating that American farmers, businessmen, workers, or other groups with special interests are becoming less articulate and forceful in singling out and grappling with problems emerging on their own fronts. Each of these groups, in exercising the right to seek economic changes in its own self-interest, carries a heavy responsibility for distinguishing between socially responsible use and abuse of its economic and political power. The vitality of the American people, the flexibility of American political and social institutions, as well as the country's past development, inspire confidence that effective and acceptable solutions to these problems will be worked out on the basis of evolving standards of desirable economic performance and conduct.

Chapter IX

Balance in Economic Growth

ECONOMIC GROWTH and stability, like productivity, do not result automatically from any "natural" law. Productivity increases require certain combinations of labor, management, capital, natural resources, and appropriate government policies. In addition, gains in productivity also depend on a steady increase in markets; and continued expansion of markets could be jeopardized by severe economic fluctuations, persistent price rises, or structural rigidities. Thus, while the promise of the American economy is very great, economic growth and stability cannot be taken for granted because of this possible threefold threat. Nor can we take for granted that our expanding economy will automatically provide the particular goods and services which will make the greatest contribution to the most urgent national objectives and the general welfare.

Alternative Uses of Potential Output

In the American economy, there are three ways in which decisions are made concerning the use of the productive resources of the nation. Consumers decide by choosing the kind of goods for which they will spend their money. Business decides the kind and amount of investment in plant and equipment and other capital goods for future production and services. The federal, state, and local governments decide, through the legislative and budget processes, the size and character of public services.

These three mechanisms are interrelated because all production, whether for consumption or for business investment or for government services, is carried out by the nation's labor force; and productive equipment and resources used for one purpose—say, consumption—cannot at the same time be used for investment or government services. Through governmental expenditure programs, credit measures, and other policies, the government can influence the manner in which a nation uses its productive resources even in a free enterprise economy. The government has the power and the means not only in authoritarian but also in democratic countries to see to it that programs are executed which have high priority for foreign policy or domestic economic and social purposes. Basically, these decisions are made by individuals as consumers and business managers through their economic behavior and by individuals as citizens through their political choices. In 1956, these decisions by consumers, business and government led to the production and consumption of $414.7 billion of goods and services. It is interesting, however, to examine some of the main purposes for which the American people allocated their resources.

Table XI

The Nation's Spending for Major Categories, 1956

	Billions of dollars	Percent of total
1. Basic consumer needs (food, clothing, shelter)	142.7	34
2. Other consumer requirements (other household items, personal business, etc.)	40.4	10
3. Transportation (user-operated and purchased)	30.3	7
4. Consumer luxuries and semi-luxuries	32.9	8
5. Education (private and public)	18.3	4
6. Research and development	7.0	2
7. Medical and hospital care	17.4	4
8. Private religious and welfare activities	4.5	1
9. Private capital investment (excl. research)	64.3	15
10. National security (excl. research)	42.4	10
11. Other government activities	19.9	5
12. Net foreign investment	1.4	—
Total national product[1]	421.7	100

[1] Total spending by major categories exceeds gross national product because research and development expenditures are here considered as capital investment items rather than as current account items. For further detail and explanation, see Appendix Table 14.
NOTE: Detail may not add to total due to rounding.

Roughly a third of the nation's expenditures went to provide such basic items as food, clothing, and shelter, with another 10 percent going for such other requirements as house furnishings, interest payments, and personal services (barbershops, legal services, insurance, etc.). It is interesting to note that (see Appendix Table 14 for additional detail) spending by consumers on luxury items such as entertainment, smoking and drinking, and jewelry approximately equaled the total combined expenditures for education and medical care (including both public and private spending for construction as well as for current operation). Also, total spending for research and development, foreign economic aid, resource conservation and development, as well as for public sewer and water programs, does not quite equal consumer expenditures for new and used cars (including the cost of their upkeep and operation). As a consequence of past restraints, serious deficiencies have developed in such important areas as education, basic research, medical and hospital care, and resource conservation. Current discussion about deficiencies in these areas is likely to result in giving them a higher priority than they have had in the recent past. This would produce changes in the allocation of resources for the various private and public purposes.

Based on long-term trends in economic growth and the allocation of resources, it is possible to make projections of the potentials of the next decade. Gross national product in 1956 prices could be approaching $600 billion by 1965—as contrasted with $415 billion in 1956. Appendix Table 15 sets forth what may be regarded to be the broad economic determinants of the next decade. It indicates that by 1965 $170 billion more goods and services could become available annually than those produced in 1956. What are the purposes for which an additional production of $170 billion might be used in 1965?

By that time, the population will have risen by 20 million. The increase in population will account for $70 billion in consumption assuming maintenance of recent per capita increases in basic needs, entertainment and luxuries, education and health, and transportation. In order to achieve this increase in total production, a rise not only in the labor force but also in plant and equipment will be needed. The necessary additions to plant, equipment, and residential construction and foreign investments require an increase year after year which might amount by 1965 to about $15 billion over and above the 1956 level. Thus, on account of the rise in population and the needed increase in plant and capacity, an additional minimum demand of $85 billion could be expected. This would still leave $85 billion additional production for which demand would have to be forthcoming.

Alternative uses of this additional $85 billion in production are possible. First is the question of the necessary level of national security expenditures. With the growth of potential production, there can be no doubt that national security expenditures could be substantially increased without impinging on a comfortable level of living and on a desirable level of capital investments. However, a relaxation of international tensions and the possibility of a reduction in armament expenditures would permit a great many other needs for resources to be met more adequately.[1]

An NPA survey of additional or expanded programs in the fields of education, health, research, resource conservation (especially water supply and utilization), highways and skyways, etc., shows a need for additional outlays of a minimum of $20 billion per year and possibly

[1] Appendix Table 16 shows alternative economic projections for 1965 assuming different levels of national security expenditures.

of as much as $36 billion (in 1956 prices) for these purposes.[2] While the additional $20 billion could be regarded as a virtual minimum, the higher figure would be within the capacity of the American economy, and would be desirable if some reduction in national security expenditures became possible by 1965. Outlays of these kinds are needed as a condition for the future growth and development of the American economy. It is in these fields that governments, particularly at state and local levels, are an important influence.

The level of living certainly could rise faster if a reduction in national security expenditures should become possible during the next decade. If the full increase of $85 billion by 1965 were made available for a rise in the level of living of wage earners and other income receivers, it would be equivalent to an annual per capita increase of close to 5 percent. However, in all of these calculations consideration must be given to the additional demands which would arise for capital equipment and the need further to expand business investment in line with the increased demands by consumers and government. Also, an increase in capital investment abroad might be envisaged for 1965.

It is most likely that the great rise in potential production would be devoted to a combination of these various purposes. It would be used to increase the level of living by a continuing rise in real wages and by wiping out the remnants of poverty. An average annual increase of perhaps 2 percent in the per capita level of living appears compatible with the expected increase in production and the necessity of making appropriate allowance for improvement of health services, education and training, research, conservation and development of natural resources, transportation, productive plant and equipment, foreign investment, and so on. When and if it becomes necessary further to increase national security expenditures, the improvement in the standard of living and in some of the nondefense areas of government services would have to proceed more slowly.

These considerations show that there are still many needed—indeed, urgent—uses for additional production. The American economy need not suffer from lack of development because of lack of opportunities for using additional products. Some people have expressed the opinion that prosperity in the United States depends on continuation and constant rise of armament expenditures. Actually, the high level of armament slows down the rate at which other desirable objectives can be attained.

Substantial shifts in any one kind of expenditures—such as a sudden increase or decrease in defense spending—may create transitional diffi-

[2] See *National Investment for Economic Growth,* a Joint Statement of the National Planning Association, SR 46, Washington, D.C., December 10, 1956, 16 pp.; also, Appendix Table 17.

culties. These difficulties, however, could be managed by appropriate budget and financial policies. Economic expansion is needed not only because steady and high employment of a growing labor force is a desirable objective, but also because the additional production of goods and services is required to satisfy urgent needs.

Economic Fluctuations

Until a few decades ago, the idea that serious and prolonged fluctuations in a free enterprise system could be prevented appeared as unrealistic as the notion that earthquakes could be prevented. For a long time, economists believed that the minimum price for a growing and free economy was economic insecurity. The best that could be hoped for was that the victims of severe, periodic fluctuations could be protected by unemployment assistance or insurance.

Classical Theory and Actuality

According to the classical laws of the market, production creates income and thereby creates the market for the goods which are produced. The theory was that production would be expanded when the relationship between prices and costs convinced the business manager that additional sales would add to profits. An economic contraction would lead to a reduction in the prices of raw materials and to lowered wage and interest rates. And this would create incentives for consumers to buy more at lower prices and for producers to employ more labor and engage in additional investments. Thus, the contraction would be quickly reversed.

Actually, these processes usually have not worked in accord with classical theory. Before a reduction in wage rates resulted in additional employment, payrolls, and demand, it more often brought about a reduction in payrolls and aggravated the contraction of purchasing power and markets. Hence, a reduction in wages, by curtailing rather than increasing markets, could defeat the purpose it was supposed to serve.

In some depressed situations, businessmen did not reduce prices and step up production, because they were not sure that price reductions would induce customers to buy more. Similarly, in such instances lower interest rates did not induce businessmen to invest more because they did not believe that there would be a market for the increased products of expanded facilities. The experience of the 1930's demonstrated that a price-cost relationship that promises profits is a condition for the expansion of business operations, but that the motive power is the businessman's anticipation of an expansion of markets. This expectation of market growth was lacking during the years of the depression.

Business at times reacts as if it expects a steady expansion of markets, despite possible temporary setbacks, and at other times as if it anticipates economic stagnation. This, in part, is a problem of psychological attitudes which involve more than purely business considerations. Consumers, for example, will at times maintain or actually increase their level of consumption, even at the cost of going heavily into debt. Such may be the case when consumers feel secure in their jobs and expect their incomes to rise. At other times, these same consumers may feel uncertain about the future job outlook and may hesitate to incur additional debts. The belief in the future prosperity of the American economy is a significant, though not the only, determinant of economic development. Business would not invest billions in new plants and equipment, people would not mortgage future incomes for housing and consumer goods, if they did not feel that the long-term economic outlook appeared favorable.

A conviction by business, labor, and consumers that serious fluctuations will be counteracted, if need be, by government action, thus, is very important in maintaining the confidence required for expansion. In the United States, as in many other countries, the people have determined that government has the responsibility for promoting conditions favorable to continued growth and for counteracting serious fluctuations. This policy, as enunciated in the Employment Act of 1946, is supported by both major political parties. The Act not only committed the government to this new responsibility, but also established executive and legislative machinery for implementing this policy. The record since the adoption of the Employment Act is encouraging. While the past decade's spectacular economic growth and relative price stability cannot be attributed mainly to operations under this Act, government policies formulated with the aid of its machinery certainly have contributed to the result.

The Forces for Expansion

In the course of America's economic development, there have been some periods when the forces making for economic expansion have been relatively strong, and still other times when they have been relatively weak. During the 1930's, when these forces were weak, it was difficult for government policies to stimulate the processes of economic expansion. During the past decade, when the forces of expansion have been strong and expectations of market growth have been high, government policies were able to operate more effectively.

Four major growth trends, in addition to a number of temporary factors, contributed to this expanding level of activity. The first is technological advance. Second is an extraordinary rise in population and family formation. The large-scale resettlement of the population in the suburbs with the consequent tremendous demand for housing, shopping centers, public utilities, and related public works is third. And the fourth major trend is the broadening of markets for durable consumer goods and homes through the extension of installment and mortgage credit. Economic expansion has been stimulated further by increasing expenditures for national defense and the expansion in defense facilities. It should be emphasized, however, that expansion in private activities took place in periods not only when national defense expenditures were increasing, but also when they were reduced after World War II, and again after the Korean rearmament.

As long as strong factors making for continued economic expansion exist, minor fluctuations can be effectively counteracted by adopting appropriate credit and fiscal policies. The experience of the past decade has proved the effectiveness of these policies *under favorable conditions*. However, this does not necessarily mean that the business cycle has been mastered or the need lessened for a readiness to counteract promptly depression and large-scale unemployment. Although strong forces for expansion are expected to continue, a number of weaknesses could appear at the same time and, by reinforcing each other, could set a downward spiral in motion. Rapid adoption of new technology and expansion of productive facilities could create temporary problems of overinvestment. In particular, rapid and widespread adoption of automation could create temporary problems of unemployment. Also, there is the possibility that residential construction one day may catch up with family formation and internal migration and that the broadening of consumer markets may reach temporary limits.

During recent years, several retardations in these factors have occurred—but fortunately not all at the same time; when one factor of growth slowed down, others moved ahead. If a number of such unfavorable developments should occur concurrently, a serious downturn in economic activities might threaten. Such a situation would pose a real test of America's ability to counteract a cumulative downturn and of the effectiveness of the government's policies to forestall serious depressions.

"Built-In Cushions" and Anti-Depression Tools

Even in the event of such an unfavorable combination of circumstances, there are good reasons to believe that the federal government, in cooperation with business and labor, would be able to prevent a serious depression of the dimensions of the 1930's. A number of "cushions," which have been built into the American economic system during the last quarter of a century, would help to reduce the speed of a downward movement.

In the past, a downturn in certain sectors of our economic life often resulted in a depression of the whole economy. Once a state of business alarm was created, depositors, fearing the safety of their deposits, would withdraw their money from the banks. The banks, in turn, would be forced to recall some of their loans—thereby creating financial problems for other businesses and spreading economic difficulties from a few to many firms and industries. Now, the fear of deposit insecurity is removed by the Federal Deposit Insurance System and similar insurance programs covering other financial institutions, such as home loan banks and mutual savings banks.

Depressions also used to spread when workers, dismissed from one industry, curtailed their spending and caused a shrinkage of markets in other industries. Today, this effect—though not eliminated—is substantially mitigated through the unemployment insurance system, which assures at least a minimum income to unemployed workers for essential purchases. Also, the provision of social security benefits would help both to maintain incomes generally, and to provide a continuing source of revenue for those aged workers who in a period of unemployment might decide to retire from the active labor force.

Another factor formerly aggravating economic fluctuations was the curtailment of expansion programs and postponement of capital expenditures until business managers were satisfied that their markets were again increasing. This attitude of businessmen has been substantially modified, as exemplified by management's long-range investment planning, which has reduced the propensity to curtail expansion programs on the basis of short-term fluctuations in sales.

Now, too, the tax system acts as a kind of automatic built-in stabilizer. If profits and incomes drop, tax payments drop too, and disposable income is not curtailed as much as total income. The government would find itself with a deficit and a part of the disappearing purchasing power would be replaced by the money which can be created through government borrowing.

Much optimism has been generated by these built-in cushions—and rightly so. However, alone they may not be enough to prevent a severe and long-lasting depression. It would be foolhardy to believe that, because of the changes in the economic structure and the mitigating factors which were not in existence in 1929-33, a depression cannot happen again. Our situation may be similar to that of a man who falls out of a window but is stopped half-way down by a ledge. If he falls from a window two floors up and is caught on the ledge after falling only one floor, he may not be badly hurt. But if he falls from the twentieth floor and is caught by a ledge at the tenth floor, it is poor consolation that he has fallen only half as far as he otherwise might.

In other words, a stabilization policy must not rely solely on built-in cushions. The government must be prepared *to act* in order to prevent a serious drop in economic activities from developing into a full-scale downswing. The government has at its command tools for combating depression.

The most readily available tool for influencing the economy is monetary and credit policy. The advantage of such policy is that it can be applied quickly, usually without need for new legislative action, and can be adapted to changing circumstances. However, the effectiveness of this tool is limited unless it is strengthened by corresponding changes in tax and expenditure policies.

In addition to the fact that tax payments would drop automatically during an economic recession, the government could reduce tax rates in order to increase purchasing power. Indeed, an important difference between the 1930's and the present is that federal taxes are so much higher now and are much more broadly distributed. This makes tax reduction in support of contracting purchasing power an effective instrument which was not available during the 1930's. Tax incentives can also be employed to induce business to engage in additional investment. Such inducements will be effective if—unlike the 1930's—there is the confidence that markets will be restored and long-term growth resumed.

Another anti-depression tool lies in the government's expenditures program. A Public Works Planning Unit has been established within the federal government. This office is charged with the responsibility of preparing advance plans for federal public works projects and of surveying state and local public works programs. While the economy has been expanding, some of the less essential public works projects have been delayed or postponed. In the event of an actual or threatening economic downturn, however, the pace of public works projects should be accelerated. To be most effective, such a policy requires advance planning on the federal level and involves close cooperation with state and local governments.

For example, a subcommittee of the Senate Foreign Relations Committee recently has considered the steps which might be needed to assure continued economic expansion in case substantial disarmament should become possible within the near future. Most of the decline in federal expenditures would be passed on to the consumers through a sizable tax reduction. However, essential nondefense projects of the federal, state, and local governments on which only slow progress has been possible in recent years could also be stepped up.

These include programs for education and health, conservation and development of resources, reconstruction of urban areas, and construction of highways and skyways. Substantial disarmament would require adjustments for a number of industries and some regions of the United States, but it should be emphasized that economic prosperity in the United States does not depend upon military requirements.

Capital exports to foreign countries, particularly to areas in the early stages of industrial development, could also be encouraged when domestic expansion slackens. This would maintain the ability of foreign countries to buy in the United States and would support production in the export industries. During the 1930's, various countries—including the United States—tried to "export" their unemployment by adopting import restrictions in order to protect their domestic markets. The consequences of this kind of restrictive policy were disastrous. Such trade policies simply transferred the readjustment burden from one country to another. However, it was soon discovered that no country was able to isolate itself effectively from the general economic decline. In such a situation, it would be more constructive if an effort were made by the industrialized countries to use their idle capacities for the mutual advantage of the less developed countries and themselves.

The problems of the business cycle, of depressions and unemployment have not yet been solved. In a free enterprise economy, where each individual independently decides where to work, what to produce, and what to consume, economic fluctuations will occasionally occur and economic adjustments will be required. However, these adjustments need not develop into depressions and mass unemployment. The American people recognize that government policies to counteract severe economic fluctuations are fully compatible with free enterprise and free labor. The determination not to let "nature take its course" signifies the final break with what in years past was a helpless attitude about depressions. Severe and prolonged depressions are not a necessity in the American economic system. They may, however, result from poor policies. The challenge is to maintain and develop appropriate policies.

The Problem of Rising Prices

Avoiding depressions is only one aspect of the larger task of maintaining balanced economic growth. Inflation is another; and it can be harmful not only to the prospects for continued economic expansion but also to the welfare of large numbers of people. During the Congressional debates on the Employment Act of 1946, it was argued that policies designed to promote full employment might engender recurring cost and price rises.

There was general agreement that an increase in wage rates commensurate with an increase in productivity not only would be compatible with price stabilization, but also would be desirable as a means of assuring the needed increase in purchasing power and consumption. However, many people feared that, under conditions of full employment, labor would demand increases in wages and other benefits in excess of productivity gains. If so, it was felt that management would grant increases, hoping that, under favorable market conditions, prices could be raised to compensate—and possibly more than compensate—for the increased labor costs. Others feared that, under favorable market conditions, business would increase prices and that labor would then demand and obtain compensating wage increases.

Some economists concluded, therefore, that full employment could be maintained only at the cost of some continued price increases. One group held the view that a moderate continued price rise would be a lesser evil than permanent or periodic unemployment. Another group contended that, as the price level continued to rise, some structural imbalances would develop and that continued economic growth might require the discipline of some permanent, or at least periodic, unemployment, or else the nation would suffer the ill effects of continued inflation.

More than a decade of experience with virtually full employment has not settled this issue. We still cannot be sure by what means a continuing price rise can be avoided under conditions of high employment. Today, prices are about double those before 1940, but this increase must be attributed primarily to the effects of World War II and the post-Korean rearmament. The general rise in consumer prices of less than 10 percent from the spring of 1951 to the fall of 1957 is not alarming, considering that over this period defense expenditures were at so high a level. Nevertheless, rising consumer prices have persisted through 1957, even when government expenditures continued on an even keel—which indicates that the problem of price stabilization has not yet been solved. The general price index would certainly have risen higher had there not been some decline in farm prices.

Government fiscal and credit policies have helped to limit the price rise, which probably would have been greater without such restraints. Some surplus was achieved in the government's fiscal transactions. The so-called consolidated cash budget (which includes operations of trust accounts and government corporations, but excludes inter-fund and noncash transactions) had a surplus in six out of the eleven fiscal years beginning in 1947. The net excess of receipts over payments amounted in that period to about $20 billion. The government in recent years successfully resisted demands for tax reduction which would have increased purchasing power and demand. Also, the government's restrictive credit policy has exerted some degree of restraint. This was particularly effective in holding down private residential construction.

In recent years, there has been much discussion about the effectiveness and fairness of a restrictive credit policy. It has a greater effect on small businesses which depend on credit than on large corporations which obtain most of their funds through internal financing. Nonetheless, an unrestrained price rise would create even graver injustices, while a much more stringent credit policy might achieve complete stabilizaton of prices only at the cost of creating considerable unemployment. In the latter case, the remedy might be worse than the disease.

Fiscal and credit measures are more effective in limiting the increase in demand than in counteracting increases in prices and costs of production. For these reasons, suggestions have been made inside and outside the government for developing policies which would supplement fiscal and credit measures to forestall inflation. More effective antimonopoly policies, flexible import policies, and some agreement between management and labor with respect to national price and wage policies have been proposed as supplementary measures for combating price rises. These are problems which must be faced in order to achieve the objectives both of economic growth and of price stability.

Mobility and Rigidity

Among the necessary conditions for the rising productivity of the American economy is a high degree of mobility; managerial talent, labor, and capital must move promptly to meet opportunities and needs as they arise. The possibility that this mobility might give way to rigidity is one of the problems which could endanger future balanced growth of the American economy. Economic mobility has several dimensions—the ease with which Americans can move among geographic areas, from plant to plant, and from one skill or career to another; the willingness of entrepreneurs to move from settled, safe enterprises to new fields of endeavor; and the movement of capital.

Geographic mobility—which has characterized the American economy over the past seventy years—is not always an unqualified blessing. Neither "boom towns" nor "ghost towns" are conducive to good community life. Workers and their families who too frequently move from place to place do not have the benefits of home ownership and participation in the political, cultural, and social life of the community. However, the fact that virtually every worker has his own automobile makes possible some shifts in his place of employment without a change in residence. If an industry in one locality declines, community life need not be adversely affected provided other industries develop in the same area and make use of the available manpower. This is what frequently happens. In contrast, there exist some continuously depressed areas where, for example, coal mines or timber stocks have been exhausted. In some of them, the development of new industries has been inadequate and labor has moved away only very gradually, resulting in relatively high local unemployment while the rest of the nation was enjoying prosperity.

Opportunities for workers to move from plant to plant within the same community are desirable but, in this respect also, complete mobility would be as undesirable as complete rigidity. It is in the long-run interest both of the firm and of the workers that steady employment be provided and the necessity of shifts from plant to plant be minimized. Seniority rights of workers, guaranteed annual wages, severance payments, and other benefits create inducements for the firm to carry a work force through the slack period rather than dismiss workers when business activities temporarily decline.

Productivity, however, is reduced if managers and labor are so closely tied to a firm that they never look for other work opportunities in which their skills may be better used. Some private pension plans tend to have this effect if pension rights are lost when the worker changes jobs.[3] However, this danger has been recognized, and various proposals have been made to overcome it. Some private pension plans already vest pension rights in the worker, who takes them from job to job. And benefits under the government's social security program are not affected by movement from one job to another.

Another type of mobility which is characteristic of the American economy is the willingness of many people to change their types of work in response to the changing needs of the market. In America, less than in most other countries, the individual seldom commits himself to an unchanging lifetime career. It is not unusual for trained engineers to accept positions as business executives; technicians to become university professors; or skilled laborers to assume supervisory functions. As more formalized training becomes necessary for most occupations, however, it is likely that people will become more reluctant to change from the type of work in which they have a previously

[3] For further discussion of the effect of pension plans on mobility, see *Private Pension Plans,* a Statement by the NPA Business Committee on National Policy, and an NPA Staff Report, National Planning Association, SR 44, Washington, D.C., December 1956, 32 pp.

acquired special skill. This may be an inevitable consequence of the technological age.

There is the possibility that new technology might also create other problems of labor rigidity. If, for example, automation should be adopted on a rapidly growing scale, it could mean that "blue-collar" and "white-collar" workers now engaged in routine operations would be replaced by machines. During the initial phase of automation, it is expected that such replacements of men by machines will be offset by the additional demand for workers in the production and maintenance of the automatic equipment. Over the longer run, also, the general expansion in the production of goods and services and reduction in hours of work might well offset some of the labor-saving effects of automation. However, a substantial change in workers' abilities will be needed, as well as retraining programs, in order to prevent the simultaneous development of a surplus of certain kinds of labor and a scarcity of other kinds.

For this reason, educational and training opportunities will assume increasing importance in a technological age if occupational mobility is to be maintained. Some businesses and unions have already initiated programs to retrain workers in industries in which automation is becoming important. A substantial number of workers are using the opportunity provided by shorter hours of work to attend special courses in order to prepare themselves for occupational advancement or for a shift from their present work. The fact that war veterans were given an opportunity for free academic training permitted a whole generation to pursue their professional interests regardless of individual financial means. In addition, many scholarships from public and private funds are given to talented students. With the veterans' educational program coming to an end, proposals for an increased general scholarship program are now getting serious consideration.

Finally, some degree of mobility of capital is also essential for balanced economic growth. As we have noted, the modern institutions of the capital market—the stock exchange, investment funds, pension funds, insurance companies, banks and other financial institutions—provide a variety of sources for investment capital. They help to channel capital into those investments which are the most promising. Nevertheless, capital mobility is far from perfect. Pension and investment funds naturally tend to favor investments in the so-called "gilt edge" or "blue chips" of the market, which aggravates the bias in the distribution of capital supply.

The most important source of capital for corporate expansion is the internal corporate funds, consisting of depreciation allowances and undistributed profits. These reserves are normally retained for the corporation's own use. Some companies with abundant capital reserves, however, have acquired through merger other firms in need of capital, and have thus increased the mobility of available investment capital. Also, through the establishment of special financial facilities, credit has been created and extended to particular areas, such as to agriculture and small and growing businesses.

In a dynamic economy, it is important that a certain degree of mobility of management, labor, and capital be maintained. If business management were assured of continued profits by protection against competition, if labor were assured of always remaining in the same job, if capital were protected against possible losses, the vitality of economic growth would suffer. It has been said that there is absolute security only in the grave. In a dynamic economy, a balance must be struck between maintaining the incentives of rewards and losses, and protecting the individual against undue hazards.

Whether the American economy can reach and cross the threshold of an age of abundance in the next decade or so depends upon many decisions and actions, economic and noneconomic, public and private. The most important economic condition for fulfilling this promise is the prevention of depression, inflation, and structural rigidity. Today, unlike the 1930's, there is a better understanding of the nature of these economic problems, and the ability and willingness to adopt effective policies and programs are much greater than in the past. If war can be avoided, there is no reason why more and more of the promise of the American economy cannot be realized in the foreseeable future.

Chapter X

Living Standards and the Distribution of Income

THE STRONG and growing desire of the people in virtually all countries for greatly improved standards of living has become so crucial a development of our times that it has been called the "revolution of rising expectations." Until the present century, mankind was reconciled to the inevitability of poverty for the masses of the people and reasonable comfort for only a small elite. Now, people all over the world reject this view. Instead, they believe that a decent standard of living, health, and education should and could be available to all. In several countries, most notably the United States, great strides have been made in realizing this objective. And yet, even in the United States, there is still a residual problem of poverty.

In America, the objective of the revolution of rising expectations is more ambitious than in most countries. Today, American workers and farmers expect—and many have already substantially attained—a standard of living which does not differ significantly in kind but only in degree from that enjoyed by the wealthier groups. In this sense, America is fast becoming a "middle-class" nation. While some class distinctions still remain, these are neither as rigid nor as humiliating as similar differences in many other countries.

The approach to a classless society in the United States has not been made by bringing everyone down to the lowest standard, but by providing more for all. The lower-income groups have enjoyed a greater proportionate increase, while the growth of very large incomes and fortunes has been curtailed. This development should not be confused with the social doctrine of equality of income for everyone; that idea never had much appeal in America. Rather, Americans primarily have sought equality of opportunity for all—particularly opportunities for education and for productive and satisfying occupations.

The rapid growth of the American economy during the past two decades has largely accounted for the substantial rise in the level of living. And if America realizes its potential for continued balanced economic growth, the standard of living of the average family in the United States by 1965 should be about 30 percent above that of today's level. Furthermore, if international tensions should be relaxed and the armament race limited, it should become possible virtually to wipe out poverty even sooner. But the economic growth necessary for eliminating the remaining poverty in the United States must be accompanied by appropriate policies specifically designed to improve further the distribution of income. Among these will be adjustments in the federal, state, and local tax systems; improvements in training, health, and social assistance programs to increase the opportunities of those in need; and adaptations of our metropolitan areas, educational systems, and other social institutions to the requirements of an approaching age of material abundance.

Residue of Poverty

Although no international standards of income sufficiency and insufficiency have yet been generally accepted, some families in the United States still have incomes that are below what Americans regard as a satisfactory level of living. Despite progress in raising such substandard income groups, some poverty—if measured in terms of American rather than international living levels—still exists, both in urban and in rural areas. In 1956, approximately 4.6 million, or 12 percent, of all nonfarm families had a total money income below $2,000. In addition, about 1.1 million, or about 22 percent, of all farm families had money incomes below $1,000.

This remaining problem of poverty in the United States, however, is different from that of the past. Until the last decade or so, the wage income of most manual workers was inadequate for a desirable level of living. Today, average wage incomes are well above the subsistence level, and families with more than one wage earner are often high in the middle-income brackets. The residual poverty is found in special situations—submarginal farming, chronically depressed areas, certain age groups, and families whose heads are unable for various reasons to work full time or at standard wage rates.

A closer look at the nonfarm families having less than $2,000 a year income underlines these differences between the poverty of the past and that which remains in the United States. The heads of over half of those families were not working owing to illness or physical handicaps, old age, or inability or unwillingness to find employment. The heads of almost 35 percent of these families were 65 years of age or older. In other cases, the heads of families were widows, or divorced or separated wives—often with children to support—who lacked the time, training, or ability to obtain full-time employment or standard rates of pay. Many low-income urban families were composed of recent migrants from economically less developed parts of the United States (particularly Puerto Ricans), who possessed few of the skills required for ordinary urban occupations. Thus, the main reason for poverty found in urban areas today is the difficulty of finding suitable employment as a result of particular personal handicaps of various kinds.

General economic growth alone cannot be relied upon to eliminate these residual pockets of poverty. Positive measures can be taken through our tax system, through economic and social programs—particularly those designed to foster increased ability to earn a living—and by adapting our institutional patterns to changing ways of life.

Taxation

A basic characteristic of the modern income tax in the United States is that it has been transformed from one levied on a small percentage of the people to one paid by most income receivers. In 1939, roughly 7 percent of the labor force filed federal income returns which were taxable. By 1955, this percentage had risen to over 65 percent owing to rising incomes, as well as to lowering of personal exemptions during the war.

Individual federal income tax rates rise from 20 percent in the lowest bracket of taxable income to more than 90 percent for the top bracket. However, since only a small portion of incomes are subject to the top rate, the effective average tax burden is lower. Also, there are a number of income exemptions and special rates (those for capital gains, for example) which reduce the actual ratio of tax payments to total income. Nevertheless, it has been estimated that people with incomes of $4,000 to $5,000 actually pay about 8 percent, while those with incomes of $100,000 and more pay, on the average, 40 to 50 percent of their total incomes to the federal government. In addition, many states and some cities impose income taxes, though their taxes, in general, are less progressive than those levied by the federal government.

If all taxes—direct and indirect; federal, state, and local—are considered, it is estimated that a tax burden of 20 percent is imposed on individuals and families with incomes of less than $2,000 and of 38 percent on individuals and on families with incomes of more than $10,000. In the highest income bracket, substantially more than 50 percent of incomes is absorbed by all levels of government. The taxes paid by families in the lowest income bracket consist largely of excise and local real estate property taxes which are included in the prices for consumer goods and rents.[1]

[1] These estimates exclude social insurance contributions. See Richard A. Musgrave, "The Incidence of the Tax Structure and Its Effects on Consumption" in *Federal Tax Policy For Economic Growth and Stability,* papers submitted to the Joint Economic Committee, 84th Congress, 1st Session, November 9, 1955, p. 98.

During the last twenty-five years, as we have noted, the income of the wealthiest 5 percent of the population has increased less than the average income. A large part of the income of this wealthiest group is derived from business profits before taxes, which have increased at least as much as wage payments. However, the combination of corporate and personal income taxes and estate taxes has limited the rise in incomes and fortunes at the disposal of the wealthiest Americans.

Indirect taxes (excise and sales taxes) play a much smaller role in the federal government's tax system than in those of other countries. However, indirect taxes are proportionally much more important in the tax systems of the state and local governments in the United States. An attempt to make the American tax system as a whole more progressive, therefore, would necessarily require a revision in the financial relationships between the federal, state, and local governments.

Some analysts of the American tax system believe that the taxes imposed on business profits and individual incomes in the higher brackets are so severe that they have undesirable effects on economical management and on incentives for investment and work. In contrast, it has been pointed out that during the last decade the relatively high taxes have not prevented a very high and sustained rate of investment, and no general lack of incentives to work, save, and invest has been noticed. Even so, tax rates imposed on business profits and high incomes are probably approaching limits beyond which their unfavorable effect on management and incentives would outweigh any possible desirable effect on income distribution.

There is considerable room for improvement, however, in the methods by which the wealthier people are taxed. The individual income tax rates for top brackets are so high that they virtually have forced the adoption of special exemptions, and thus have led to what has been called "the erosion of the income tax system." Proposals have been made to reduce the top rates of the income tax, while eliminating some of the special income exemptions and the loopholes, as well as making the estate tax more effective. The same groups, under this proposal, would continue to pay approximately the same amounts of taxes, but in a more desirable and equitable fashion.

Since by far the largest share of the total national income accrues to people with the lower and middle incomes, it follows that the huge government expenditure programs cannot possibly be financed by taxes imposed only on the wealthiest. This is illustrated by the fact that the total amount of the annual incomes before taxes of persons reporting $20,000 and more is estimated at $20 billion to $25 billion, while total annual expenditures of federal, state, and local governments exceed $100 billion.

There is the possibility that, with economic growth, the federal government's tax revenue will rise by more than its expenditures, particularly if a limitation in the armament race should become possible. Substantial tax reduction then would become feasible. Such a change would certainly include a reduction both of income taxes in the lower brackets and of excise taxes. Thereby, the disposable income of most Americans would be increased. However, a problem results from the fact that, as far as nondefense programs are concerned, the greatest increase in expenditures has taken place in the state and local governments, and the tax resources of these governments are limited. If state and local taxes were raised while federal taxes were reduced, the tax system as a whole would become less progressive. Some re-examination of the division of functions and revenue sources among the federal, state, and local governments therefore appears necessary.

Considering all aspects of the tax structure, it seems clear that a substantial additional reduction in the inequalities of income is not likely to result from making the tax system considerably more progressive. Improvements in the distribution of incomes must depend primarily on continued economic expansion and the provision of increased opportunities and services for the families at the bottom of the income pyramid, both in urban and in rural areas.

Economic and Social Welfare Programs

The main beneficiaries of the additional resources provided by economic growth, as well as by the heavy taxation of middle and higher incomes, have been the numerically large groups with lower incomes. Indeed, policies concerned with the redistribution of incomes have been designed more with the aim of raising those at the bottom than of lowering those at the top of the income scale.

Both recent economic developments and special government programs have helped to improve the ability of low-income families to increase their real incomes in various ways. For example, in the expanding American economy, full-time and part-time employment opportunities for women have been growing and the wage disparity between men and women has been narrowing. Women are taking advantage of these opportunities; the proportion of the female population, fourteen years and over, in the labor force rose from 26 percent to about 33 percent between 1940 and 1957. Women are better able to work because of increased facilities for day care of small children and the fact that most families can now afford to buy labor-saving household equipment.

Other examples are found in the varying responsibilities assumed by the federal and state governments for emergency and permanent programs to help those in economic distress as a result of illness, old age, physical disability, loss of jobs, and other causes. Not only has there been a steady increase in the number of people under unemployment insurance and social assistance programs, but also many are eligible for benefits under commercial health and hospital insurance plans and the rapidly increasing pension and welfare programs financed by business firms, trade unions, and benevolent associations.

Table XII

Private and Public Insurance and Pension Programs, 1940-1956

(Number of employees covered, in millions)

	1940	1945	1950	1956
Public:				
Old-Age and Survivors Insurance	35.4	48.3	46.4	68.0
Unemployment Insurance	25.1	29.0	34.8	38.9
Private:				
Pension Plans[1]	3.7	5.6	8.6	16.5[4]
Commercial Group Insurance[2]				
Life insurance	n.a.	11.5	19.4	35.0
Hospitalization	n.a.	4.4	10.1	16.7
Surgical	n.a.	4.0	10.3	17.4
Medical	n.a.	.5[3]	3.5	10.1
Accidental death and dismemberment	n.a.	4.5[3]	8.1	17.3
Temporary disability	n.a.	7.1	15.1	20.8

n.a. Not available.
[1] Excludes annuitants.
[2] As of December 31st.
[3] 1946.
[4] 1957 estimate.

SOURCES: *Statistical Abstract of the United States, 1957;* Department of Labor; Department of Health, Education, and Welfare; Institute of Life Insurance.

Despite the tremendous growth of these public and private insurance and pension programs, current benefit plans do not yet provide adequate protection for all against many of the social, economic, and physical hazards of life. Both the public and private systems, however, can be expected to expand in some balanced relationship with increases in wages, business investments, and government services. As productivity continues to rise, these programs can be extended to more people and their benefits made more nearly adequate without undue strain on the American economy.

Where the persistence of poverty is largely the result of economic factors beyond the individual's control, specific governmental programs are being undertaken to remedy conditions. Among these are special government programs designed to rehabilitate the so-called "marginal" farmers by enabling them to acquire additional land, better seeds and fertilizers, mechanical equipment, and technical advice, or to shift to part-time or full-time industrial occupations. Special problems also are posed by families living in economically backward parts of the United States or in local communities where economic life is depressed owing to changes in the location of industries, in consumer tastes, in competition from newer substitutes, products or production techniques, and so on. In the past, these pockets of depression were regarded as merely local problems; the government could help only to the extent that the affected workers qualified for unemployment insurance and general assistance programs. In a few of these localities, businessmen, on a voluntary and cooperative basis, have pooled their resources and converted existing idle facilities for new uses. In most cases, however, the problems cannot be solved by local efforts alone. Therefore, in recent years depressed areas have come to be regarded as a legitimate concern of the federal government, and various legislative proposals are pending for authorizing the government to assist depressed areas in attracting new industries and new employment opportunities.

Finally, there are public policies which indirectly help large numbers of Americans to increase their earning capacity and their ability to consume. These include the free or subsidized services and facilities provided by the government in such fields as general education, vocational training, public health and hygiene, recreation, low-cost housing, veterans' benefits of all kinds, and many others. Measures designed to prevent discrimination because of race, sex, religion, or place of birth also tend to raise incomes and living standards.

Private Philanthropy

In addition to the many kinds of programs financed by federal, state, and local governments, there are numerous other activities financed by private sources which are designed to raise the levels of living and improve the quality of life. Totaling over $7.5 billion in 1956, these efforts are collectively called "private philanthropy." The term philanthropy covers all voluntary contributions by individuals and business corporations, as well as the expenditures of private foundations and charitable trusts, for the support of private, nonprofit institutions and activities in the fields of religion, social welfare, health, education, scientific research, the arts, etc.

The magnitude and diversity of private philanthropy is a unique feature of the American system. Giving is not mainly an activity of the wealthy, and virtually all American families contribute to the support of welfare, health, and educational activities. A notable development of the past decade has been the growth of donations by business corporations to local welfare agencies and hospitals, nationwide health organizations, educational institutions and scholarship programs, museums and cultural activities, and research institutes both in the natural and the social sciences.

Table XIII

Estimated Source and Allocation of Private Philanthropy in the United States, 1956

	Millions of dollars	Percent of total
Source:		
Contributions from individuals	$5,172	69
Contributions from business corporations	510	7
Charitable bequests	237	3
Private foundations[1]	600	8
Income from capital (except foundations)	1,000	13
Total	$7,519	100
Allocation:		
Religious agencies (including church-related educational and welfare activities)	3,760	50
General welfare agencies (domestic and overseas)	1,730	23
Education (primarily higher education)	977	13
Health agencies	676	9
New endowments of foundations	226	3
Miscellaneous purposes	150	2
Total	$7,519	100

[1] Adjusted to eliminate duplication with sums reported in other items but given through foundations.
SOURCE: F. Emerson Andrews, *Philanthropic Foundations*, Russell Sage Foundation, New York, 1955; p. 18, revised by author to 1956 estimates.

Many institutions and activities which in other countries are dependent upon financial support from the state or from an endowed or established church are in the United States wholly or partly financed by such voluntary contributions from individuals and business firms. Moreover, in the United States, voluntary giving is deliberately encouraged by tax incentives. Individuals pay no federal income taxes on the portion of their incomes contributed to *bona fide* philanthropic activities provided it does not exceed 20 percent of their total income otherwise liable to taxation (an additional 10 percent is also tax exempt if contributed to religious and certain educational activities). Business corporations may contribute up to 5 percent of their net income before becoming liable to the federal corporate income tax.

Today, tax exemption for individual and corporate giving is justified on the grounds that it helps to maintain the private and decentralized character of decision making and initiative and to sustain the self-reliance of local groups and communities. This encourages freedom and diversity and increases the chances that promising new ideas in science, education, and welfare will be supported. Thus, as a necessary complement to government programs and activities, private philanthropy makes a very significant contribution to improving the level of living and the quality of life in the United States.

Changing Ways of Life

The unprecedented rise of the level of living over the past two decades, combined with the rapid growth both of population and industry, have resulted in major changes in the ways of life of Americans. Not least of these are the changes in location of the places where people live and work. Factories and homes have been moving out of the cities and into the countryside. With the improvement of roads and the ownership of automobiles by about three out of every four American families, people need no longer reside near their jobs. In consequence, residential sections have mushroomed in the suburbs and nearby rural areas while the cities themselves have grown only slowly, if at all. A recent estimate of the population of New York City, for example, actually indicated a decline of over 100,000 inhabitants from 1950 to 1957 owing primarily to the movement of families to the suburbs. These changes are creating special difficulties for the cities and metropolitan areas.

Relative to the rising amount and cost of the services and facilities they are expected to provide, the cities have not been able to expand their resources fast enough. Already, and increasingly in the years to come, the cities of America face critical problems of redefining their functions; reconstructing their obsolete or inadequate streets, structures, and services; and redesigning their municipal institutions and finances. The latter problem is especially important, and its solution may well involve the development of novel administrative and financial arrangements embracing both the older cities and the newer, expanding suburbs.

The city governments and local political groups have been slow to anticipate emerging problems and to adopt effective measures for coping with them. In default of adequate public initiative, private groups in a number of localities have begun to study the nature and magnitude of these problems and to devise practicable solutions. These growing movements for urban redevelopment are usually composed of mutually cooperating businessmen, trade unionists, and professional people, who are also becoming active in seeking solutions to the problems of the schools and of other social institutions confronted with major changes in the size or nature of the functions they have to perform.

Another major contemporary change in the way of life of Americans is a direct result of the economy's greatly increased productivity and spread of automation. Americans now have to spend far less time at work than in the past; and there is no question that they will have more and more leisure time as the American economy continues to grow.

The reduction in the hours of work to the present average of forty per week, as well as the lessening of physical strain and drudgery of many jobs, has already resulted in a rough division of the day into one-third working time, one-third leisure, and one-third sleep. Particularly in industries with a full-time work week of less than forty hours, many workers have been increasing their incomes by taking part-time secondary jobs. As real wages continue to rise, however, this practice should become less common. Indeed, the growth of productivity may be so great as to make double jobs undesirable. Hence, waking time not used for economically productive work is bound to increase, amounting perhaps to 40 percent or more of the day. In addition, an even greater increase in leisure time probably will occur through longer vacations and retraining periods, and perhaps ultimately by a further reduction of the present standard five-day work week to four days.

Throughout human history, only a small, favored fraction of mankind has had the wealth and time to pursue constructive forms of leisure. Many of the greatest advances of civilization are owed to the so-called "leisure classes" who were able to develop talents in the arts or knowledge of the humanities and sciences. The daily life of the great mass of the people in America—as in most of Western society—traditionally has been oriented toward work and the struggle to satisfy material wants. Whatever leisure time was available tended to be considered only a necessary period of "re-creation" to enable further work to be done.

Some doubts have been expressed that Western civilization is culturally prepared for substantially shorter hours of work, with resulting longer hours of leisure. During his working day, man's activities are largely determined by the task which is put before him. For his leisure, his activities are also determined to some extent by the needs and obligations of his family and community. However, there is a greater freedom of choice in the use of leisure than during the work period. And freedom of decision always involves the possibility of misuse of that freedom.

Whenever in the past a reduction of the work week was considered, someone always expressed concern that more leisure would only mean more hours for bars, dance halls, gambling, or family squabbles. Actually, these fears have proved largely groundless. This is partly because many workers undertook additional jobs, but more important has been the fact that the reduction of the work week has been occurring when earnings were rising and the mode of living of the worker was changing. For example, with the move to a house of his own the worker has found more incentive for a pleasant and constructive use of his leisure time in gardening and home improvements.

The "do-it-yourself" movement not only was a response in the early postwar years to shortages of consumer goods and, more recently, to rising prices of services, but it has been an adjustment to mass home ownership and increased leisure time. It also is an effort to satisfy on a mass scale what Thorstein Veblen called "the instinct for workmanship," the desire for self-expression through the creative work of one's own hands. In addition, there has been a tremendous expansion of other leisure-time hobbies and handicraft activities, and in many forms of active sports and outdoor recreation. An indication of this is readily seen in the vast national and state parks which, in season, are pressed to capacity by a multitude of campers, fishermen, and nature lovers; and in the expanded sales of recreational and sports equipment.

Some Americans—not without reason—tend to be somewhat discouraged about the outlook for the more contemplative uses of leisure time—the enjoyment and creation of music, drama, books, and of other nonprofessional participation in the arts, humanities, and sciences. In their opinion, existence of a vast and steadily growing audience for the mass entertainment and communications industries holds a danger that more and more cultural offerings will be designed to appeal to the lowest common denominator in intelligence and taste. And they point to symptoms of such possible cultural recession often found in movies, radio and television programs, popular magazines, and newspapers. They warn, too, that a possible corruption of taste may result from certain types of mass advertising.

But encouraging signs are also found throughout the country that more and more Americans are taking advantage of opportunities for cultural growth. Through radio and television, for example, operas, symphonies, and plays have reached people who had never before heard, or had scoffed at, "classical" music, drama, and comedy. Programs dealing with literature, art, history, science, and public affairs generally are also stimulating the interests of a growing number of Americans. Cities and towns across the land with privately financed symphony orchestras and chamber music ensembles are already numerous and continue to increase, along with the mounting sales of high-fidelity equipment and long-playing recordings of good music. More and more cities have their own professional repertory theatres, and amateur dramatic groups are legion. Innumerable Americans paint or sculpt nonprofessionally, and on weekends and holidays the museums and galleries are thronged. The large and still growing sales of good fiction and of scholarly books in paperback form have been one of the major cultural developments of the past decade. Anyone who takes the trouble actually to investigate popular culture in the United States will find it vigorous and varied, even if not always of the highest quality.

Nevertheless, one of the greatest challenges confronting Americans in the coming decades is to adapt their educational system not only to train more and better scientists, technicians, and skilled workers, but also to develop the individual's potentialities for participating in the expanding opportunities for cultural growth and for constructive recreational activities in the approaching age of abundance.

Improving levels of living generally and raising the level of low-income families are not only accepted social objectives in the United States, but are also economic necessities. American industry depends on growing mass markets. Even if it were socially desirable, rising consumption of the high-income groups would not create enough outlets for the expanding industrial capacity.

It has sometimes been suggested that an overriding priority should be given to raising productivity and that the expansion of welfare is of secondary importance. In reality, these are not incompatible alternatives but complementary necessities. In a healthy democracy, welfare measures are essential for promoting productivity, while growth in productivity makes possible the expansion of well-being for all. Trouble arises when one is emphasized at the expense of the other. This is why a socially responsible and mutually cooperative attitude on the part of businessmen, labor unions, farmers, and government officials is essential to maintaining the necessary balanced relationship between rising productivity and increasing welfare. Otherwise, economic growth slows down, and continuing demands for rising living standards can be satisfied only by largely futile efforts to redistribute a fixed national income. The net result may only be to exacerbate social tensions and cause further damage to the national economy.

The United States has simultaneously achieved a substantial rise in productivity and a substantial increase in living standards. If a proper balance is maintained and economic growth continues, there is every reason to believe that poverty resulting from inadequate incomes will cease to be a significant problem in American society within the next decade or even earlier.

Chapter XI

Concentration of Economic Power in American Industry

THE IMPORTANT ROLE both of large and of small corporations and of their managements in raising the level of productivity in the American economy was discussed in Part One. But we left unanswered the question of whether American ideals of democracy and free competition have been sacrificed for the sake of the technological and managerial achievements of the large corporations. This is not a new question. Through much of American history, people have asked it and sought answers through various types of legislation.

Today, some Americans believe that concentration of economic power is not compatible with the decentralization of political and economic decision making that is essential for the survival of democracy. More than any other, the issue of concentration dramatizes the apparent clash between the Hamiltonian ideal of national power and wealth and the Jeffersonian ideal of personal independence and self-responsibility. We believe, however, that a practical reconciliation of these partially conflicting principles is beginning to emerge.

The Degree of Concentration

To what degree do the large corporations actually dominate American industry? Several different methods of measuring economic concentration have been developed.

One of the measurements of the relative importance of large corporations is found in figures on the "100 largest manufacturers." In 1947, the 100 largest manufacturing corporations accounted for 23 percent of production by all manufacturing industries; but by 1954, the same number of companies accounted for 30 percent of production (measured by value added by manufacturing).

Another type of measurement attempts to depict the "ratio of concentration." It has become conventional to speak of a high ratio of concentration if the four largest companies in an industry account for 50 percent or more of the industry's total shipments. Industries of medium concentration are those in which this ratio is between 20 and 50 percent and those of low concentration have a ratio of less than

20 percent.[1] The motor vehicle industry is, for example, a high-concentration industry, as measured by the fact that the largest four corporations in it provide 75 percent of all motor vehicle shipments in the United States. Between 1947 and 1954, the high-concentration industries increased their share of total product shipments from 25.7 percent to 26.9 percent—a modest increase, but an incease nevertheless.

While the importance of the large corporations and the ratios of the high-concentration industries both show some rise in recent years, the number of industries with high rates of concentration has not increased significantly. This apparent paradox is explained by the fact that industries in which large enterprises dominated and which always had a high ratio of concentration happened to be industries which have grown faster than those with lower rates of concentration.

Thus, a conclusion as to whether economic concentration has been growing slightly or remaining unchanged in recent years appears to depend in part on the method of measurement; in no case has the change been very substantial.

Despite the relative importance of the large corporation in American industry, most employees still work in more or less decentralized industries rather than in industries of high concentration. In the low-concentration industries, 6.3 million workers were employed in 1954. This was roughly 40 percent of the total employment in manufacturing industries. Industries with a medium degree of concentration employed 5.7 million, or 36 percent of total manufacturing employment; while 3.9 million, or 24 percent employed in manufacturing industries, worked in industries of high concentration. Thus about three-quarters of the manufacturing workers are employed in industries of low and medium concentration.

In such industries as textiles and apparel, wood and wood processing, and printing, no significant concentration has taken place. Also, small units predominate in some of the service industries—for example, there are about 30,000 motels along the highways of this country. Over 500,000 establishments—more than 50 percent of the total number of service establishments—are operated solely by persons who are self-employed. Thus, there is still a wealth of opportunities in the United States for people who want to be "their own bosses."

These figures refute the exaggerated notion that American industry is dominated by a few large corporations. Nevertheless, the fact remains that the large corporations are very important in the most dynamic industries and that in these industries competition among the few is more typical than competition among many producers. This situation is a source of real concern.

---

[1] Appendix Table 18 presents the concentration ratios in selected American industries as well as explanatory notes containing qualifications which must be considered in the use of these figures.

Reasons for Concern About Concentration

The classical philosophy of private enterprise is that, in a free competitive economy, no enterprise is likely to become dominant in any industry. If one corporation is so profitable that it can expand, competitors are likely to enter the field. In addition, it was assumed that there is an optimum size beyond which the efficiency of an enterprise would decline and costs rise. A system of free and competitive enterprise thus was considered to be a system of decentralized economic power.

In some European countries, the severity of the competitive struggle has been mitigated by cartel agreements among the firms in a particular industry. In the United States, antitrust laws have been designed to prevent this type of restraint of trade, and cartels exist only in a few exceptional cases which have been specifically permitted by legislation. Cartels also run counter to the dynamic spirit of American entrepreneurs, who do not like to be limited in their struggle for expansion, even by self-erected barriers. This reaction was evident following the demise of the cartel-like "code authorities," which were created for various industries in the early phases of the recovery efforts of the 1930's. Objection to that kind of organization was one of the main reasons why the Supreme Court's invalidation of these organizations found general acclaim, both inside and outside business circles.

The virtual absence of cartels in America does not mean that competition in the American economy works in accord with the classical doctrine. Contrary to classical expectations, a few very large enterprises dominate the market in some of the most important industries, and great difficulties are faced by newcomers who challenge the entrenched positions of the giants.

If these giants are successful in the competitive struggle and contribute so much to the rise in productivity, one may well ask why they cause concern. At least five major reasons are advanced for worry over the emergence of a few giants in several branches of industry:

1. Although there is really no monopoly as long as there are several competing enterprises in one industry, competition among the few has a different character from competition among the many. Prices in industries with a few leading firms—which have been called "administered" prices—are not the same as those determined by hundreds of competitors. Hence, there is opportunity to maintain or raise prices beyond what would otherwise be determined competitively.
2. The investments of a few hundred large enterprises make up a large percentage of total private gross investments. These, too, may be called "administered" investments. They are determined

largely by expectations of business managers, and in turn have a great influence on the actual level of economic activity.

3. With giant enterprises, many thousands of executives, engineers, scientists, and other employees, as well as thousands of so-called "independent" dealers and millions of consumers become dependent on one enterprise. The possibilities are thereby narrowed for choosing among firms for whom an individual wants to work, among products a dealer wants to sell, and among goods a consumer wants to buy.
4. There is the possibility that very large enterprises can impede entry into the market by smaller enterprises, even if the latter could be more efficient in production. Large enterprises use their financial superiority in a variety of ways—by embarking on advertising campaigns which are beyond the financial reach of smaller competitors, by "temporary" price wars, by exclusive arrangements with dealers, and so on. Also, patent pools have been arranged which permit a number of established firms to use each other's patents but do not grant the newcomer the same privilege. These possibilities of abuse of economic power are to a large extent, but by no means completely, limited by the enforcement of antitrust laws.
5. Concentration of economic power also implies the possibility of exerting an undue amount of political power.

Bigness and Monopoly

Economic power, like all forms of power, carries the opportunity for use and for abuse. Naturally, the best policy would be to combat abuse of power without depriving the economy of the usefulness, high efficiency, and rising productivity contributed by large enterprises. In seeking to eliminate abuses, however, there has been a tendency to confuse the problems of large enterprises with those of monopolies. While these problems are interrelated, they are not identical. In conventional thinking, monopolies are prevented if a number of producers serve the same market and try to undersell each other by offering products at a price at which all potentially profitable production could be absorbed by the market. We have pointed out that in many industries, including retail trade, this type of vigorous price competition is not only surviving but probably has become even keener in recent decades. And in some industries, competition has been modified, emphasizing differences in quality, design, and credit terms more than differences in prices.

In addition, another type of competition has been evolving. It is the competition that railroad transportation meets from highway and air transportation, which is effective in spite of the high rate of concentration in the railroad industry. It is the competition between copper and aluminum in supplying material for electric transmission lines. It is the competition which steel as a building material will sooner or later meet from plastics strengthened by radiation; and oil and gas from nuclear power. It is the competition which the small retailer meets from the chain store, the cooperative, and the mail-order house. This is the kind of competition which can be promoted most effectively by technological advances or innovations in management techniques.

One of the most dramatic price reductions in economic history—when Ford's Model T went into mass production—resulted not from competition in the conventional sense but from a technological and managerial innovation. Effective as this kind of competition is, it is significant only in the longer run. It remains true that at any one time some industries—for example, steel or chemicals—can still determine prices within a rather wide range. Particularly in industries with relatively inelastic demand, enterprises can increase profits, or at least not reduce profits, by setting their prices higher than necessary for a strictly competitive price. However, in such industries prices will not be raised beyond the point where they would—in the long run—encourage the development of substitutes. Within the range fixed by costs of production at the lower end, and by the competition of substitutes at the upper end, prices in these industries are not determined automatically by market conditions; they are determined by decisions of business administration. That is what economists mean when they speak of "administered" prices.

In setting the actual price within the economically determined limits, responsible businessmen must take into consideration a variety of other factors, including the effect of price policy on public opinion, on possible antitrust action, on collective bargaining, on long-term market prospects, and so on. Thus, an economy in which large enterprises are important poses problems of economic policy which are different from the problems that existed when prevention of private monopolies and maintenance of competition were regarded as the main objectives. Before considering those differences and their implications for policy, it may be useful to take a brief look back at the development of American antitrust legislation.

Antitrust Legislation

In 1787, Jefferson urged that Americans include an antimonopoly provision in the new Constitution. Long before federal antitrust legislation was finally adopted, many states had antitrust and antimonopoly laws on their statute books. In the main, however, these state laws were more significant as expressions of popular fears of the concentration of economic power than as deterrents to monopolistic practices. It was not until the Congress passed the Sherman Antitrust Act in 1890 that the federal government began to acquire the authority needed to combat monopolistic practices. This authority has been strengthened and adapted to changing conditions and problems by additional laws, including the Clayton Antitrust Act of 1914 and the Anti-Merger Act of 1950.

The antitrust laws of 1890 and 1914 were designed primarily to prevent "practices in restraint of trade"—that is, actions on the part of large corporations, individually or in collusion, which enabled them significantly to reduce competition in an industry, to dominate the market for a product, or to raise prices in the absence of increases in costs. At first, the courts did not enforce the law of 1890 vigorously. But a series of Supreme Court decisions beginning after the turn of the century marked the start of more stringent applications, which were extended by the Act of 1914. Since then, the antitrust laws have been more effectively enforced, particularly in cases where a producer has tried to eliminate competitors or attempted in other ways to dominate the market. Occasionally, action has been taken even before evidence of actual monopolistic pricing of products.

To some extent, the antitrust laws have been interpreted as though they were designed to prevent not an actual but a potential restraint of trade. Such a potential might lie in mergers or other means of increasing the size of a large corporation relative to its industry or market. This use of the antitrust legislation has been confirmed and strengthened by the Anti-Merger Act of 1950, which was passed in response to the growing number of mergers among large corporations since World War II. These business mergers of recent years have raised new problems and have revived old controversies regarding the aims and administration of antitrust policy.

There are a number of industries which for reasons of economy or safety cannot be left to unregulated private competition. These are public utilities—such as railway, highway, and water transportation; electricity and gas; telephone, telegraph, radio, and television communication. Whereas in many countries, government monopolies have been established in all or most of these industries, in the United States most of them are privately owned and managed but under government supervision. Exceptions are some municipally owned public transport systems, the federal postal system, and some government-owned facilities for the production and distribution of electricity, usually as part of multiple-purpose river development projects.

Federal and state regulation of privately owned utilities is designed to restrict competition, which could be harmful in these industries, and to assure adequate service for the consumers. Such supervision of private utilities has both advantages and disadvantages, if contrasted with the alternative of government ownership and control. On the one hand, avoidance of large government enterprises appears as an advantage to most Americans. The need of government supervision, on the other hand, has the disadvantage that various private interests often try to influence the decisions of the regulatory agencies. In some instances, it is claimed, the regulatory agencies not only prevent wasteful duplication of effort in such fields as transportation, communications, and power, but also shield the established companies against wholesome competition. However, any deficiencies of this nature in the regulatory agencies are subject to criticism by the Congress and the public and to correction in response to such criticism. Whatever may be the merits and demerits of various methods for dealing with public utilities, most Americans have favored government supervision of privately owned and operated corporations in preference either to unregulated private operations or to nationalization of these public utilities.

Corporate Structure and Performance

At present, the whole philosophy underlying antitrust attitudes and government regulation of business activities is being re-examined, largely in response to recent important changes in the nature of corporate enterprise and business mangement.

As a result of the increasing recognition of the constructive role that the corporation plays in the American economy, there is today less demand than formerly that the antitrust laws be used to restrict the size of the corporation and limit "bigness" *per se*. The American public, including the trade unions, is reconciled to the fact that big corporations are here to stay. That does not necessarily mean, however, that antitrust legislation will become less important.

The considerable change now occurring in public opinion with respect to corporate size is prompted by a number of factors. There is not only increasing recognition that competition among the few can be as keen as competition among the many and awareness of the importance of interindustry competition. Also, the belief that size alone may lead to consumer exploitation has been diminished because of the realization that large enterprises mean mass production for mass consumption with large unit volumes and, usually, with relatively small unit profits. And there are few remaining fears that corporate owners or managers will build up fabulous personal fortunes out of monopolistic profits. Moreover, the more equitable distribution of income and wealth among Americans of virtually all social groups has been concurrent with the growth of large corporations. The notion that concentration of production must be accompanied by concentration of wealth in fewer and fewer private hands has been disproved by the fact that corporate ownership, especially of the large corporations, is widely dispersed among a great many stockholders. Moreover, while the relative importance of large corporations was increasing, the percentage of total disposable income of the wealthiest Americans was declining.

Also without much contemporary validity is the old conviction that the smaller firm is inclined to treat its workers more humanely than the large concern. Today, labor's ability to obtain a fair wage and favorable working conditions does not depend upon the uncertain benevolence of humanitarian employers. It is much more solidly based upon the bargaining power of strong trade unions, the socially responsible labor relations policies of most business management, and the minimum standards enforced by government regulations. In general, wages and working conditions in large corporations are at least as satisfactory as in small ones; and such fringe benefits as retirement pensions and health services are usually greater, owing to the more ample resources of large corporations and their advantages in obtaining group insurance.

These changes in the attitudes toward bigness have brought about some changes in the decisions of the courts in interpreting the antimonopoly laws, and further shifts are likely to occur.

Two criteria have always been used for deciding on the need for antitrust action—the structural standard and the performance standard. The structural criterion relates to corporate size, mergers, and other types of intercorporate affiliations. Taking antitrust action on the basis of the structural criterion assumes that corporations which are very large and supply or control a large share of the market are likely to have engaged in monopolistic practices. Thus, exclusive reliance on the structural standard tends to penalize corporations which have built up their economic power through superiority of their products or organization. This tendency has occasionally resulted in antitrust action, not against actual monopolistic practices, but against bigness as such.

In contrast, it has been argued more recently that a large corporation need not in itself be bad as long as its economic power is not abused. This view stresses the performance criterion, that is, the test of whether economic power is actually used constructively or harmfully. It seems to us that the performance test is likely to be increasingly emphasized, even though it creates a number of difficulties in adjudication. One of the tasks still to be solved is the development of applicable standards for distinguishing between the productive use and the abuse of economic power. As such standards are developed, the relative importance of the structural criterion—that bigness is in itself harmful—will probably decline still further.

These changing attitudes toward corporate size do not mean, however, that the courts as yet regard the structural criterion as unimportant. Only recently, the Du Pont interests were ordered to divest themselves of their General Motors stock. The Supreme Court did not charge any undue influence by Du Pont in General Motors; but it stated that this affiliation *could* be misused, thus reflecting a structural, rather than an actual performance criterion. Nevertheless, it is likely that the emphasis in antimonopoly procedures will shift increasingly to the performance test, that is, the actual misuse of economic power. Already, there is slowly emerging an "unwritten code of corporate performance" concerning what is and what is not in the general interest

Corporations are in business to make profits, and making profits indicates that their products are produced and marketed efficiently. However, production and sales efficiency are not the only factors by which profits and corporate performance are, or should be, determined. Managers of corporations are increasingly recognizing that making profits also requires both good employee relations and good public relations. Good public relations, in turn, makes it necessary for corporations to consider the impact of their activities on the economy as a whole. True, the government agencies entrusted with the enforcement of the antitrust laws will take action when violations are evident. But, equally important in reducing the abuse of economic power is the fact that the corporation operates in a "fishbowl." Public and Congressional scrutiny—of price policy, for example—can often be more effective than antitrust procedures through the courts. Indeed, the performances of large private corporations in America are sometimes more carefully watched than are those of government corporations in some countries with nationalized industries.

Perhaps most important of all in reducing abuses have been the changes, which we have already discussed, in the nature of corporate management itself. The growth of business management as a career and the evolution of the modern corporation into an entity with a life of its own have led to the passing of the "public-be-damned" attitude of some of the old "captains of industry." There are today strong pressures on the corporation and its managers for socially responsible attitudes in the conduct of their businesses.

Even though all of these important influences are working against the abuse of power by giant enterprises, opportunities and impulses for monopolistic abuses are nonetheless still operative. These grow out of the desire to eliminate unwanted or annoying competitive pressure, particularly making it difficult for additional firms to enter the market;

the desire to use economic power for political ends; and other expressions of the inherent shortcomings of human nature and society. Thus, even recognizing the constructive role of corporate enterprise and the increasingly responsible attitude of most corporate managers, the government will still need to watch corporate performance and to step in when abuses of economic power occur.

Fewer Americans today would favor an antitrust policy which would carve large, efficient enterprises into pieces simply because they represented a concentration of economic power which *might* be abused. Conversely, few Americans would wish to abolish the government's antitrust responsibilities as a means of preventing *actual* abuses of economic power. The great majority of Americans, including most business leaders, accepts the fact that in a democracy power must be accompanied by accountability. In the modern large corporation, the direct control of individual stockholders is often weak and ineffective. It is true that no one will invest in a corporation unless he believes that it has an efficient management which will result in a rising value of the stock and in a satisfactory yield. Nevertheless, managers often could exercise their corporation's power without accounting for its use to anyone other than themselves were it not for the existence of government antitrust policies and of public scrutiny. Through these means, the exercise of corporate power ultimately becomes accountable to the American people.

Small Business Policies

Antitrust policy is essentially negative, designed to prohibit abuses. By contrast, the problems of small and medium-sized businesses must be attacked with positive policies and measures. These are, however, primarily the responsibility of the businessmen themselves, and government programs can and should only supplement and foster the necessary initiative and energy on the part of those firms adversely affected by changes in their competitive environment.

The survival problems of small and medium-sized businesses result from a variety of factors which, singly or in combination, can cause serious deterioration in a firm's competitive position in its industry. Some of these factors arise from the advantages of big corporations. But there are other factors responsible for the plight of many small firms which have nothing to do with the competition of large corporations. Probably the most influential is the unwillingness of many firms —and sometimes of their workers as well—to adapt to technological changes, which have made either their products or their production methods obsolete even in industries where there are no giant competitors. Changes in consumers' tastes and in locational advantages also have had substantial effects, as in the cotton textile and men's hat industries. Of less significance is the competition of imports, for much of the adverse effect alleged to result from "cheap foreign labor" often really arises from the unwillingness of some American firms to improve their lagging productivity, their outmoded products, or their obsolete sales and distribution methods.

Insofar as the deteriorating competitive position of small and middle-sized firms results from their own unwillingness to abandon obsolete products and methods, there is nothing that the government can do to remedy the problem. In these cases, such government measures as loans, subsidies, protective tariffs, and other forms of assistance only treat symptoms and not causes, and usually perpetuate the difficulties they are supposed to eliminate. For such cases, only educational efforts might be effective. In contrast, there are many other small firms which are willing to make necessary changes but lack the financial means or the freedom of action to do so. For this type of firm, appropriate financial and technical assistance by the government can provide the missing elements required to make the company's own initiative and enterprise effective.

Government policies also can assist small business generally in overcoming some of its handicaps in competition with larger firms. The crucial weakness is of a financial nature. A number of programs have been adopted for the purpose of making credit available at favorable terms to promising business firms. The results of these programs are encouraging, but it cannot be said that the most appropriate form for small business financing has yet been found. There might be a need for a semi-public chain of small business finance institutions, parallel to existing semi-public farm credit organizations. Legislation for setting up such financial institutions has been discussed in the past and is now again under consideration.

With respect to certain other weaknesses, small business is finding its own ways of adjustment. For example, small businesses cannot engage in research and development programs of the size conducted by large corporations. In consequence, consulting firms are being established which make their facilities and talent available to small companies having ideas for, but no means of undertaking, large or long-term research programs. Also, some of the states and some voluntary organizations of businessmen have adopted "technical assistance" programs for small business.

Another way by which small firms have sought to overcome their disadvantages of size has been by mergers among themselves. This movement is distinguishable from the better-known mergers of large corporations during the past decade. In some of these mergers of small firms, the identities of the constituent companies do not disappear, and a certain degree of freedom of action is retained by each within the framework of the new combination. Many of these mergers have been successful in enabling the enlarged firm to obtain greater amounts of capital at more reasonable rates, and in other ways have added new strength to the combined enterprises.

Most significant, there are important fields of activities in which small business has proved its superiority over large and giant enterprises. It is by searching out such opportunities that small business has survived in the past. The future of small and medium-sized business will also depend primarily on the ingenuity and alertness of individuals. Government aid cannot substitute for these characteristics, but can only come to their support.

Thus, both by changing policies designed to prevent the abuse of economic power and by new measures for helping small enterprises, the American people are gradually working out a reconciliation between continued economic growth and the preservation of freedom and initiative. In this process, old concepts of "monopoly capitalism" are rapidly losing their validity in the light of the far-reaching changes that have occurred during the past two decades—both in the nature and effects of large companies and in the competitive situation of small firms. It is still too early in this reappraisal to foresee in detail the new attitudes and policies likely to emerge. But it is important to clarify further the kinds of business conduct which at the same time meet the long-range needs of stockholders, employees, and consumers, and also contribute to the effective use of resources and to economic growth and stability. A fuller development and articulation of such rules of conduct is one of the most important conditions for using economic power as a vehicle of economic growth.

Chapter XII

The United States in the International Economy

THE INTERNATIONAL ECONOMY of the mid-twentieth century consists of a few industrialized nations with high productivity and high standards of living, and too many other countries which still have a long way to go in their struggle to raise consumption for growing populations above mere subsistence levels. These countries in the early stages of industrial development—comprising the vast majority of mankind—need and are seeking imported goods and capital to hasten their development, and many of them have turned to the United States to satisfy their requirements. However, most of these countries encounter both external and internal obstacles in their efforts to obtain desired quantities of American products and American capital:

1. A great many countries are unable to earn through the sale of their exports sufficient dollars to pay for the goods they would like to buy in the United States. Although the United States is the largest importing nation in the world, the amount of goods and services which it buys abroad is quite small compared to its own domestic production.
2. Even though the United States is the largest exporter of capital in the world, most potential American investors feel that investments in domestic enterprises are more profitable and safer than foreign investments. This is because investments within the United States are reasonably secure from the uncertainties of the international situation and from the nationalistic suspicions of foreign investors found in numerous countries. As a result, many countries desperately needing additional capital for development purposes are unable or unwilling to obtain it from the world's remaining large private capital exporter.

Since the end of World War II, the United States and, to a lesser extent, international organizations have adopted extraordinary measures to help many countries balance their trade accounts and develop their economies. The urgency for such measures did not arise simply because of extensive war damage; rather, it has arisen from more fundamental changes which have been taking place in the international economy. The solution to problems created by these basic changes is not only of economic importance, but may also be of decisive political significance. It is not an exaggeration to say that domestic economic achievements may come to naught unless these international problems can be more effectively tackled.

International Trade Patterns and Problems

The usual international trade pattern is for advanced industrial countries to be large net exporters of manufactures and large net importers of raw materials. The pattern for underdeveloped countries is the reverse—large net exporters of raw materials and large net importers of manufactures. Though a key member of the international trading system, the United States does not fit either side of this pattern. It occupies the unique position of being simultaneously the world's largest importer and largest exporter, not only of crude and semiprocessed raw materials but also of manufactured goods.

Until the twentieth century, the American economy primarily exported agricultural and industrial raw materials and imported man-

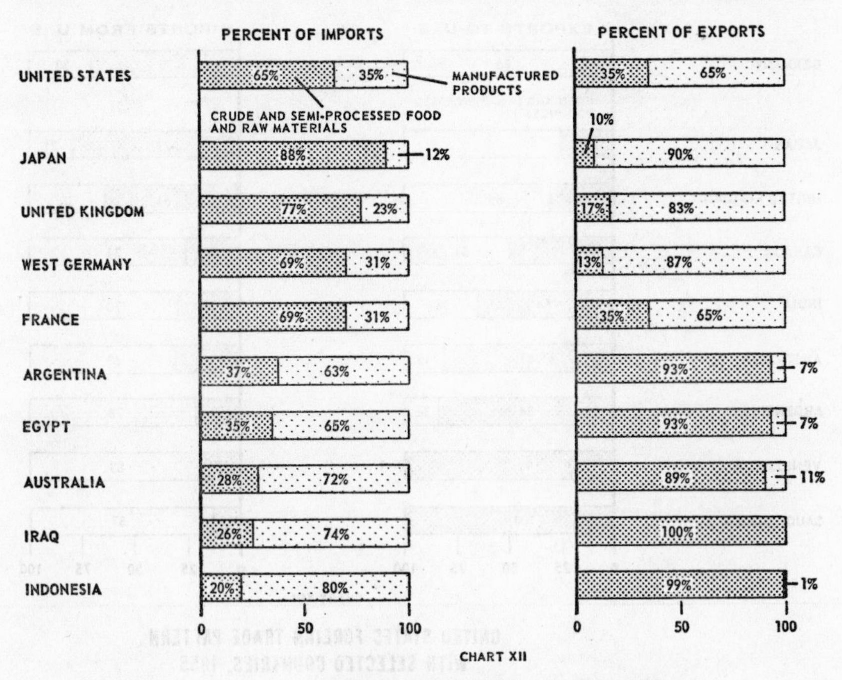

CHART XII

INTERNATIONAL TRADE PATTERNS, 1955

Source: Yearbook of International Trade Statistics, 1955, United Nations, New York, 1956.

ufactured goods. But even when its industrial production overtook and greatly surpassed its output of primary products, the American economy did not cease to be a large exporter of agricultural commodities and, to a less extent, of industrial raw materials. The high agricultural productivity in the United States, which provides far more than is needed to satisfy the requirements of Americans, has enabled the United States to become the world's residual supplier of such agricultural goods as cereals, meat, and other foodstuffs, animal feeds, cotton, tobacco, and forest products. Despite the growing dependence of American industry on imported metals and minerals, exports of certain industrial raw materials and fuels also are still important. American exports of these crude and semi-processed materials have risen rapidly and substantially whenever alternative nondollar sources of supply could not meet expanding world demands. At the same time, American exports of manufactured goods have been even greater and continue to grow.

The dual character of the American economy in world trade can be seen most clearly in the composition of its exports to, and its imports from, different parts of the world. Vis-à-vis the less developed

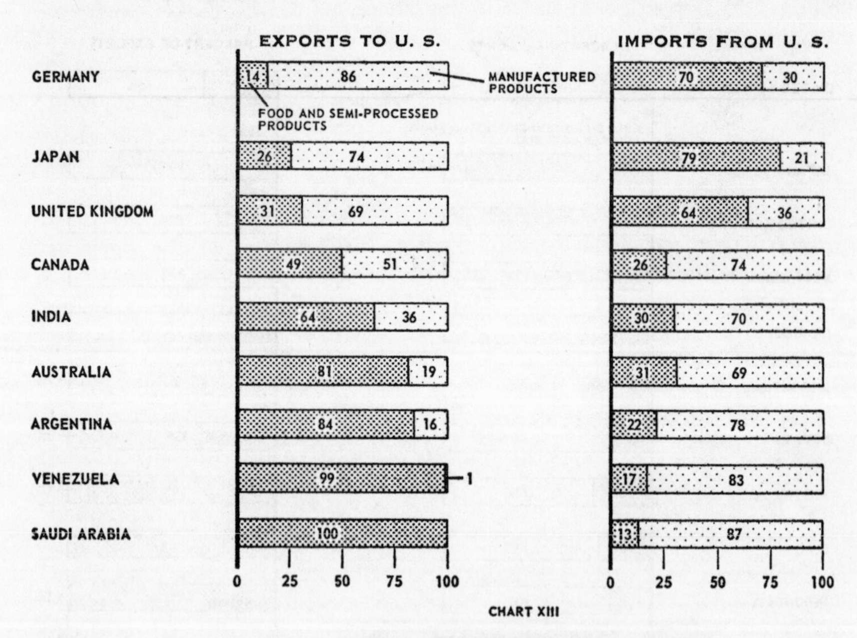

CHART XIII

UNITED STATES FOREIGN TRADE PATTERN WITH SELECTED COUNTRIES, 1955
(in percent)

Source: Yearbook of International Trade Statistics, 1955, United Nations, New York, 1956.

areas, the United States is an advanced industrial country, importing mainly their primary products and shipping to them mainly manufactured goods. Vis-à-vis the industrial nations, the pattern is reversed.

From the point of view of the rest of the world, trade with the United States is of vital importance. Exports to and imports from the United States amount to well over half of the foreign trade of many countries, and constitute a very significant element in their economies. In total, the United States is the world's single largest market and source of supply; American exports and imports amount respectively to about 19 percent and 13 percent of world exports and imports. In contrast, trade with the rest of the world is in the aggregate of comparatively minor importance to the American economy. Imports of goods and services are below 5 percent, and exports are below 6 percent, of the U. S. gross national product.

It is, however, only in the aggregate that imports and exports are of relatively minor importance to the American economy. Certain tropical agricultural products—such as coffee, cocoa, natural rubber, hard fibers, bananas, and certain hardwoods and vegetable oils—cannot be grown economically in the United States. Nonferrous metals and minerals—such as manganese, chrome, nickel, copper, bauxite, tin, and diamonds—either do not occur in the United States or cannot be produced in sufficient quantities at reasonable costs. Conversely, some American industries depend significantly upon export markets—motion pictures, most types of industrial and agricultural machinery, transportation and electrical equipment, and others.

Nevertheless, in the aggregate, the United States is today only marginally dependent upon foreign trade, while the rest of the world is vitally dependent upon its trade with the United States. This situation is responsible for the need for and the difficulty of achieving and maintaining a high level of balanced trade between the United States and the rest of the world without undue restrictions against dollar purchases by the latter.

The discrepancy in relative importance of international trade arises from the differences in the size, diversity, and productivity of the American economy compared with the economies of other countries. Because of the advantages of mass production, the diversified industrial products of the United States can be offered at prices and in quantities with which foreign industries find it difficult to compete in the American market. These characteristics also make American goods very attractive in foreign countries. But, many of these countries do not earn enough dollars to allow unrestricted imports from the United States. Hence, for the last two decades, most countries have limited their imports of American products by such devices as exchange controls, quotas, and tariffs.

For the future, there are factors which will tend to increase the U. S. dependence on the world economy and improve the ability of other countries to trade with the United States. As the population and production of the United States continue to rise and its own resources are further depleted, American industry will be more dependent upon new sources of raw materials. Continued improvements in the levels of living of the growing population will also tend to increase American demand for those manufactured consumers' goods and quality foods and beverages which comprise the bulk of U. S. imports from Western Europe. In addition, American tourists probably will continue to spend more abroad than foreign tourists spend in the United States. Meanwhile, the countries of Western Europe will increasingly be moving toward unification of their economies, thereby enjoying more of the benefits to productivity of belonging to a large, diversified, and growing market. Thus, as both the less developed and the industrial countries raise their living standards and increase productivity, they should, over the long term, be able to earn more dollars and thereby reduce their restrictions on dollar imports.

Other factors, however, may partially offset these trends. Population is increasing all over the world, and hence import needs—particularly for food, fuel, and industrial raw materials—may increase for other countries as well as for the United States. The rise in industrial production and living standards in the less developed countries might prevent adequate increases in their export of food and other raw materials. If import needs for raw materials should increase faster than the growth of the international market for manufactured exports, then payments problems could persist, particularly for the industrialized countries of Western Europe and for Japan.

On balance, the net effect of these trends and counter-trends is likely to work in favor of a mitigation of international trade problems. But the outcome does not depend solely upon such long-range economic developments. American import policy—particularly the tariff—has been, and will continue to be, an important factor.

In a large number of industries, particularly those in which mass production methods predominate—such as most consumer durables—American manufacturers do not fear foreign competition in the domestic market. And these industries could expect to sell more of their products in foreign markets if other countries did not restrict or prohibit dollar imports. In contrast, there are some American industries—most of them labor-intensive, relatively small-scale, or making specialty products or complex equipment not mass produced—in which foreign competition is keen in the domestic market. These include textiles, watches, chinaware, certain chemicals, and large specialized electrical and other heavy equipment in which the engineering and labor components are high. American producers in these and similar industries have already obtained, or seek, protection against actual or potential foreign competition in the domestic market through tariff increases, quota restrictions, preference in government procurement contracts, and other means.

Except during the administrations of President Grover Cleveland and President Woodrow Wilson, American tariff rates rose steadily after 1860, and reached their peak in the Smoot-Hawley Tariff Act of 1930. Since then, the trend has been downward—primarily as a result of the Reciprocal Trade Agreements Program. Originated under President Franklin D. Roosevelt and continued to the present, this program has not only substantially lowered the rates on many articles, but has greatly increased the list of imports on which there are no, or only nominal, duties. However, in most cases rates have not been cut below the point where substantial foreign competition with domestic products would be likely to occur. In addition, there have been legal procedures—among them, the so-called "peril-point amendment" and the "escape clause"—by which producers who believed themselves hurt by foreign competition could seek to prevent proposed tariff reductions or obtain increases in rates previously reduced.

A few years ago, the slogan "trade, not aid" was often heard, both in the United States and in other countries. Its proponents meant to imply that if the United States were to abolish all of its import barriers, there would be no need to provide dollar aid to allies and friends abroad. This view rested upon a misconception of the capacity of the American economy to absorb imports and of the ability of its trading partners to increase exports. Moreover, there are some countries whose dollar-earning exports, even in the best of circumstances, would be too small to finance necessary and desirable imports from the United States.

Some economists have argued that the inability of many countries to import freely from the United States is a temporary and exceptional phenomenon, resulting in the early postwar period from war damage and more recently from the effects of rearmament and economic development programs. Postwar reconstruction has done much to reduce the dollar deficits of many European countries. However, given the economic and political conditions of the mid-twentieth century, the concern for defense and for progressive economic development will continue to dominate the economic objectives of most countries. While the size of expenditures for these purposes can and does vary with changing conditions and means, substantial resources will be devoted to them for the foreseeable future. More fundamentally, it seems unlikely that relatively small modifications in the levels of government expenditures in many countries could eliminate the deep structural discrepancies between their economies and that of the United States.[1]

While American import policy is not the whole—or even the major part—of the solution to international trade problems, it is nonetheless a significant factor. Considering the predominance of protectionist sentiment in the United States from the 1860's to the 1930's, the progress made during the past two decades in liberalizing American import policy is noteworthy. Moreover, should there be another serious economic recession in the United States, there is good reason to believe that relief would not be sought, as in the early 1930's, by efforts to "export" unemployment through large-scale increases in tariff rates and other devices designed to restrict imports and force exports. Nevertheless, the future of American import policy is more uncertain today than it has been for many years. Producers who are, or believe themselves, adversely affected by the competition of imports are becoming better organized, more articulate, and more skillful in pressing their case for tariff and quota protection. In contrast, producers dependent upon imported materials or export markets, consumers generally ,and others, who benefit from increased or lower-cost imports—though numerically a very much larger group—are amorphous and less effective politically than they used to be. Hitherto, the knowledge that a liberal import policy is an important part of American foreign policy has served to keep alive the trade agreements program and to bring about some reduction of other import barriers. Whether this momentum can be maintained in the future or whether protectionist views will increasingly prevail is an issue still to be resolved by the American people. A favorable outcome depends upon maintenance of balanced economic growth in the United States and upon finding alternative ways of meeting the legitimate needs of domestic groups and communities that would be adversely affected by further lowering of import barriers.

Capital Exports and International Investment Policy

In conventional economic theory, nineteenth-century England provides the classical model of the relationship between an advanced industrialized nation and the world economy. Until World War I,

[1] For an analysis of these structural problems of the contemporary international economy see *The Political Economy of American Foreign Policy,* Report of a Study Group Sponsored by the Woodrow Wilson Foundation and the National Planning Association, Henry Holt & Company, New York, 1955, 414 pp., Part I (German translation published under the title *Weltwirtschaft und Weltpolitik,* Verlag fuer Geschichte und Politik, Wien, 1957).

Great Britain supplied the rest of the world with manufactured goods and, under its free-trade policy, readily took the world's raw materials in payment. The excess of British exports over British imports was financed by the investment of British capital in plantations, mines, factories, and public utilities in many other countries, particularly those of the British Empire. From 1815 to 1914, world trade depended upon the availability of British banking, shipping, and insurance services, and the pound sterling was the virtually universal medium of international exchanges. During those years, the London money market provided most of the short-term credits needed for international commerce as well as the long-term funds required for capital investment. In short, it was this special position of England as the organizing center of the nineteenth-century world economy which enabled goods and money to move with such freedom across national boundaries and made possible the operations of the international gold standard system.

Early in the twentieth century, British industry was overtaken or surpassed by that of the more recently industrialized countries, particularly the United States and Germany. In consequence, England lost its pre-eminent position in the world market and was eventually forced to abandon its free-trade policy. At the same time, in country after country, universal suffrage had spread, along with a growing conviction of the great mass of the people that their economic security and welfare could be substantially improved. Thus, it gradually became impossible for national governments to permit the level of employment, the distribution of income, and the standard of living to be determined automatically by the inexorable workings of international market forces and the severe disciplines of the gold standard. Since 1914, two world wars and the intervening depression, the advent of many new nations, formerly colonies, and the rise of aggressive totalitarian empires have dealt the final blow to that integrated, freely trading world-wide economic system.

Though the world economy of the nineteenth century has vanished beyond recall, many still regard it with great nostalgia, and conventional theories of international economics continue to be based upon it. This is the reason it is often claimed, both in the United States and in other countries, that if the United States would only act like a "creditor nation" (that is, like England before 1914), there no longer would be any problem of financing desirable levels of international trade and investment. Such a view is the financial counterpart of the "trade, not aid" fallacy, and its proponents argue that the United States must abolish its tariff barriers and must offset any remaining excess of exports over imports by investing an equivalent amount of capital in other countries. Even assuming that world political and social conditions were not insuperable obstacles, this prescription would be mistaken because it overlooks an essential difference between the contemporary American economy and that of nineteenth-century England.

In the United States, private investors have neither the need nor the inclination to invest capital abroad on anything like the relative scale of the British before 1914. By the middle of the nineteenth century, the British economy had largely outgrown its food and raw material base, and had to invest growing amounts of capital in the development of overseas supplies, first for its own industries and later for those of other countries as well. These needs provided opportunities for larger profits than could be earned in many kinds of domestic investment, and hence capital funds flowed abroad via the London money market, not only from English investors but also from wealthy individuals in other European countries. Nor were foreign investments believed to be significantly more risky than domestic ones in the apparently tranquil world of the nineteenth century, policed by the ubiquitous British navy.

Today, American investors have ample opportunities for profitable investments at home, and the need to develop overseas sources of supplies is still limited to a relatively small number of minerals, metals, and tropical agricultural products. More important, the safety of domestic investment is very much greater than that of capital invested abroad. The dangers of war, revolution, and nationalist extremism, combined with current restrictions on the movement of goods and money, have discouraged private investors from entrusting their funds abroad. Although private American investment abroad is larger than that of any other country, it is nevertheless small compared with the requirements for capital funds of the many nations now struggling to accelerate their economic growth.

The largest proportion of private U.S. investment abroad is in Canada and Latin America, particularly in petroleum and manufacturing. This concentration graphically illustrates the present limited incentives for Americans to invest abroad and the relatively greater security of investment in the Western Hemisphere. Elsewhere, too, private American investment is concentrated mainly in the petroleum industry of the Middle East and in manufacturing industry in Western Europe, particularly the United Kingdom.

Since World War II, the U.S. government has tried to stimulate greater private American investment abroad by a variety of means. These include special tax benefits, guarantees of the convertibility of earnings and capital into dollars, and information services for investors interested in overseas possibilities. In addition, the government has negotiated investment treaties with other countries, under which each pledges to accord equality of treatment to the other's investors, to eliminate double taxation of earnings, and to provide adequate com-

Table XIV

Private Direct U. S. Investment Abroad, 1956

Industry	Canada	Latin America	Western Europe	Other countries	Total	Percent by industry
		(Billions of dollars)				
Petroleum..........	1.8	2.2	1.0	2.2	7.2	33
Mining and smelting	.9	1.1	[1]	.3	2.4	11
Agriculture.........	[1]	.6	[1]	.2	.8	4
Manufacturing.....	3.2	1.5	1.8	.5	7.1	32
Trade.............	.4	.5	.3	.2	1.4	6
Public utilities.....	.3	1.2	[1]	1	1.7	8
Miscellaneous......	.8	.3	.3	.1	1.5	6
Total............	7.5	7.4	3.5	3.7	22.1	100
Percent by regions..	34	33	16	17	100	

[1] Less than $50 million.
NOTE: Detail may not add to totals because of rounding.
SOURCE: Department of Commerce, *Survey of Current Business*, August 1957, pp. 22–30.

pensation in the event of confiscation or nationalization. However, the number of such treaties is still small.

Other countries are beginning to provide more favorable climates for private foreign investment than in the early postwar period. This is especially true of many of the newly independent countries, which were originally very suspicious of private foreign investors because of unfortunate experiences under colonial rule or doctrinaire nationalistic or socialistic objections. In part, this friendlier attitude is the result of their own pressing need for development capital and the difficulty of obtaining adequate amounts either from domestic sources or from other governments and international organizations. In part, too, it stems from a growing recognition in many less developed countries that responsible private American investment is not only a very efficient means of obtaining needed capital and technical and managerial knowledge, but that its activities can also bring increased economic and social welfare to large numbers of people. In recent years, the record of American companies in significantly improving living standards and health and educational levels of employees and their families in many foreign countries has helped importantly to overcome fears of possible "exploitation" and to refute charges of "imperialism." [2]

Despite the more receptive attitude of other countries and the efforts of the U.S. government to encourage overseas investment, pri-

[2] See NPA's series of case studies of individual American companies operating abroad, published under the general title *United States Business Performance Abroad.*

vate investment is not likely to play a role comparable to that in the nineteenth century. Not only is the total magnitude of private capital exports on too small a scale, but private funds are not usually invested in certain types of activities essential to economic and social development. In contrast to the nineteenth century, a country's basic transportation facilities, public utilities, and health and educational services today are not likely, in most cases, to be financed by private investment. But such facilities and services are preconditions for stimulating the investment of private capital in agriculture, mining, manufacturing, and distribution.

Private American investors are able to accomplish only a part of the function which the international flow of capital should fulfill in the mid-twentieth century. How an adequate flow of development capital can be achieved is one of the major persisting problems of the next decade both for the United States and for the capital-importing countries.[3]

Foreign Economic Programs and Policies

Since the end of World War II, the U. S. government has provided about $65 billion of aid to other countries to enable them to buy the goods and services needed to rebuild their war-damaged economies, to improve their national defense, and to accelerate their economic growth. Government-financed loans and grants have been necessary because, as we have seen, the ordinary international exchange of goods and flow of capital were inadequate to provide many countries with sufficient resources to accomplish these purposes without extraordinary help. In addition, U. S. contributions to international organizations—such as the United Nations agencies, the International Monetary Fund, the International Bank for Reconstruction and Development, the Organization of American States, etc.—have provided more than $3.5 billion for international use.

Americans have been willing to transfer such sizable funds to allies and friends abroad for a variety of reasons. Most obvious has been a direct national interest in preventing economic collapse or communist conquest or subversion in countries important to the security and prosperity of the United States. But this motive of self-interest has been combined with a humanitarian impulse to help the sufferers from natural or man-made disasters anywhere in the world, and to share American wealth and skills with less developed countries.

[3] For an analysis of the problem and suggestions for its solution, see Raymond F. Mikesell, *Promoting United States Private Investment Abroad,* National Planning Association, PP 101, Washington, D.C., October 1957, 87 pp.

In the last few years, some of the countries which received American aid in the earlier postwar period have achieved substantial economic recovery and a fair degree of internal political stability. In addition, the kinds of aid characteristic of the past dozen years were by intention and nature temporary and exceptional, and their indefinite continuation has made them increasingly irksome to donor and recipients alike. In consequence, questions have been raised both at home and abroad about the future of foreign aid, particularly for nonmilitary purposes. But, though some of the gravest dangers have receded as a result of past economic aid, the ordinary international flow of goods and capital has not been restored to adequate levels. Nor is the end yet in sight of the need to help allies and friends strengthen their defenses against the Soviet and Red Chinese threats and accelerate their economic growth.

In these circumstances, a new concept of American economic aid and technical assistance to other countries is required. Such a concept can only be evolved on the basis of a clearer understanding of the nature of world economic problems and of the general objectives toward which the foreign economic activities of the U. S. government should be directed. Fundamentally, the problems of the international economy arise from the profound political, social, and economic transformations which have been occurring since 1914.

In Western Europe, the nineteenth-century prerequisites for successful national existence—industrial and commercial pre-eminence, military supremacy, colonial rule, and politically weak and economically inarticulate working classes—either have already passed away or promise soon to do so. Since World War II, these countries have been trying to reconstruct their political and economic life on a new basis. Novel forms of shared sovereignty and unified markets promise greater security and higher productivity and living standards for the European countries willing and able to participate in these new arrangements. Whether the efforts toward European unification will succeed cannot yet be foreseen. But the outcome for good or for ill will be a fateful one for the future of democratic societies. Hence, the United States is vitally concerned.

Many noncommunist countries of Asia, Africa, and Latin America are undergoing an even more profound transformation than that of Western Europe. Awakened from centuries-old patterns of social and economic activity by the impact of Western trade and ideas, these countries are no longer able or willing to return to their former modes of life. Some have recently achieved political independence, and virtually all now passionately seek to accelerate their economic growth so as to raise the living standards of their people. But, neither rising productivity nor higher living standards can be attained in most of the less developed countries without far-reaching changes in their existing economic systems, and in their inherited cultural values and social institutions. Such evolutionary changes are difficult and take time.

Moreover, for many of these countries, the process of social change is complicated by two important factors. One is the ceaseless efforts of the Soviets and the Red Chinese to extend their domination by every possible means. The other is the rapid rate of population growth which has largely resulted from the introduction of Western medical science and economic technology. In consequence, the development and use of resources must be accelerated sufficiently to make possible adequate defense against communist conquest or subversion and increases in production in excess of population growth.

The noncommunist countries engaged in this gigantic process contain nearly half of the world's population and possess the largest reservoir of as yet untapped natural resources remaining on this planet. The outcome of changes occurring on so vast a scale cannot but have major consequences both for the people of these countries and for the United States as well. American concern with this process is not simply one of assuring adequate development of raw materials on which to draw for future import needs. More significantly, Americans have a vital interest in the future of these countries because of the importance of narrowing the great disparity which now exists between the latter's low productivity and living standards and those of the nations which are farther along in industrialization. No new system of international political and economic order can be built in a world where the gulf is permitted to widen between the few countries of growing abundance and the many struggling desperately with poverty and over-population.

Thus, the United States is vitally concerned with the current transformations both in the European nations and in the less developed countries. The American hope is that these transformations will not threaten the maintenance and progress of Western society in general and of American democracy in particular. This does not mean that other countries are expected to adopt or imitate the characteristic values and institutions of American society. Practically, Americans cannot, and morally should not, dictate the kinds of economic and social systems they would like others to have. Rather, it is only that the attitudes and institutions of these emerging new societies, no matter how different, should be of a kind that Americans can live with peacefully, trade with to mutual advantage, and cooperate with constructively in the solution of international political and economic problems.

The new attitudes and institutions now evolving in countries throughout the world will and should be products of the choices their peoples make for themselves within the limits of their political and economic capabilities and cultural potentialities. Compared with these factors, America's foreign economic activities are quantitatively of only marginal significance, at most. But, nonetheless, they may have considerable importance in two respects.

The first is by providing these countries with an increment of financial resources and technical skills which—small though it may be—can often make the decisive difference between the success or failure of economic development programs. The second is through the numerous opportunities afforded by these foreign economic activities for Americans and other peoples to live and work intimately and constructively together, here and in other countries, in real-life situations which are meaningful and important to both. Continuous, practical, day-to-day relationships among peoples of widely different racial and historical backgrounds provide the best—perhaps the only—way by which mutual trust and understanding are developed, skills are assimilated, and techniques are adapted across cultural barriers in a voluntary fashion. In this way, Americans can serve as examples of functioning democracy in government and in the economy.

The economic development and social transformation of these countries will not be accomplished easily or completed quickly. Hence, American concern and participation in this process is likely to continue for the foreseeable future. The foreign economic activities of the United States need to be regarded as a continuing and integral part of American foreign policy, directed primarily toward achieving long-range, positive goals rather than merely preventing immediate dangers. Otherwise, a secure and progressive international system is not likely to evolve.

A more positive approach to foreign economic activities requires changes in form, method, and organization. Hitherto, for example, American assistance to other countries has mainly taken the form of nonrepayable grants. This was desirable so long as funds were needed to rebuild war-damaged economies and help restore some measure of internal political stability. But in the future, economic growth and development will in one way or another improve the ability of recipient countries to make some kind of return for the financial help received from the United States. Moreover, both abroad and at home, there is a growing desire to have a larger and more prominent element of mutuality and reciprocal benefit in the relationship. Many recipient countries are becoming increasingly disturbed by the inferior status and the indefinite moral obligation implied by their continued acceptance of nonrepayable grants. As a result, it is desirable for most transfers of funds from the United States to other governments to be loans, whose terms, conditions, and forms of repayment would be fitted to the particular capabilities of each country.

Though there have been periodic reappraisals of the U. S. government's foreign economic activities by the Executive Branch, the Congress, and private institutions and groups, as yet little has been done to adapt the form and methods of these programs to changing attitudes and needs in the United States and the recipient countries. Fundamentally, the problem will only be solved when Americans and their allies and friends recognize that progress requires partnership. In a successful partnership, the parties not only respect each other's independence and dignity but also willingly assume and conscientiously discharge mutual responsibilities and obligations. New and more effective ways need to be found in the coming years for carrying out this partnership principle.

Difficult international problems have to be solved in building the kind of world economic and political order which is conducive to the security and progress of all free peoples. In this continuing task, the American people have a special obligation because of their strength, their wealth, and their relative freedom of action. The economic aspect of this task is to integrate the American economy more fully into the international economy so as to make possible adequate levels of trade and capital investment. This cannot be done by nostalgic attempts to reproduce the vanished conditions of the pre-1914 era. It can only be accomplished by means which recognize present realities and prospective needs and which take adequate account of changing values and expectations throughout the world.

The progress made to date in adapting American foreign policy to the new conditions of the mid-twentieth century seems astonishingly rapid and far-reaching when viewed from the vantage point of the isolationism that prevailed until World War II. But the question remains whether the changes have been sufficient to cope effectively with the needs of the times. Americans still tend to think too much in terms of traditional concepts of nationalism and sovereignty. While they recognize the relevance for other countries of new approaches to international cooperation, partnership, and shared sovereignty, they have as yet been unwilling to apply fully the underlying logic of these creative ideas to their own responsibilities and requirements. Americans tend also to be too impatient of the slow resolution of international difficulties. They often fail to recognize that problems beyond a nation's borders are inherently more difficult to tackle than purely domestic ones, particularly when a country is committed to democratic methods. Finally, Americans too frequently fall into the error of regarding the imperialistic ambitions of the Soviet and Chinese communists as the sole cause of contemporary world problems. Great and growing as the danger of Russian or Red Chinese aggression and subversion may be, a miraculous elimination of it would still leave deep-rooted and difficult international problems, though their solution might be pursued with less haste and improvisation. Indeed, the communist menace is largely the product, not the primary cause, of more fundamental changes and trends in world population, expectations, and capabilities. These provide communism with its opportunities and means, and in turn communism raises the underlying problems to critical degrees of urgency.

Though the further changes needed in American foreign policy have been increasingly evident for several years, it was only in the fall of 1957 that they became apparent to most Americans. Russian successes and initial American setbacks in launching guided missiles and space satellites—and the reactions of allies and friends abroad to these developments—have provided a salutary shock which has shaken implicit American assumptions about the scientific superiority, national security, and international prestige of the United States. Out of the ensuing reappraisal of all aspects of America's position in the world, there could eventually emerge a new, more inspiring, and more vigorous fulfillment of America's responsibilities to help build a better world order in which all peoples can some day enjoy both secure freedom and increasing welfare.

Chapter XIII

The American Economy: Nature and Outlook

WE HAVE LOOKED at the American economic system from many sides. We have pointed to remarkable achievements; we have discussed deficiencies and unsolved problems. Perhaps the most significant accomplishment has been that alert criticism, which flourishes in a democracy, has stimulated a continuing search for constructive solutions and remedial actions.

The American economic and social system of today has undergone many changes and is substantially different from what it was twenty-five or fifty years ago. But there has been no sharp break with the past, as in countries which have experienced social revolutions. In the United States, inherited institutions have been adapted to fulfill new functions. Here, the emerging economic and social system confounds the observer who tries to characterize it by using traditional names, such as capitalism or socialism. The American economy does not operate in accord with any of the "pure" laws of laissez-faire capitalism or of socialism. Nevertheless, it operates very effectively—probably more effectively than either of those pure systems could.

In these concluding pages, we attempt to summarize the nature of the American economic system. In a sense, this is an impossible task, because the most characteristic feature of the American system is that it is not fixed, but a living thing, moved by many—in part conflicting—impulses. By looking at some of the characteristics that have made it work in the past, however, it is possible to discern the directions in which the American economy is most likely to move.

American Individualism and the Role of Government

Perhaps the most basic fact in the American economy is that the people working in shops and factories, in offices and laboratories, in homes and on farms, feel that they, as individuals, are an integral part of the American system. Neither business managers nor workers nor government officials are regarded as the sole movers or even the most important factors in the system. Each has his indispensable role to play. Nor is his role one that is imposed by superior authority. Rather, it is evolving, open to criticism, and subject to change.

In their jobs and in their daily life, the American people are striving for their own and their families' happiness. But they are convinced that by seeking their own advancement they are also serving a common purpose—the interests of the community as each one conceives them. These sometimes conflicting impulses do not lead to anything like "class conflicts." Instead, they are more or less effectively resolved either directly, as in labor-management relations, or indirectly through the day-to-day political life of the nation. This is possible because the American system is based on a deeply rooted bond by which conflicting interests and aspirations are held together. Although difficult to define, this bond is the essence of American democracy.

The feature of the American economy hardest to comprehend is that it combines individual freedom and initiative with a high degree of organizational management. What might on the surface appear as a basic contradiction in objectives or attitudes is reconciled in the American pattern of life. In spite of the industrialization and urbanization of the past century, some elements of the frontier spirit of an earlier age have survived. This spirit combined a strong sense of self-reliance with a ready willingness to join in cooperative efforts when the need arose. Both attitudes still have their creative places in the American economy. Even in the largest factory or office, the worker never becomes a mere number; he always remains Mr. Smith or Mr. Jones—or more likely, Bill or Bob. This is more than a mere mannerism. It reflects an enduring respect for the individual—which explains, in part, the high productivity of American labor.

All through these pages, we have emphasized the absence of dogmatic solutions and the persistence of the spirit of trial and error in which difficulties are tackled as they arise in the light of the relevant facts and real alternatives. One example is the very flexible dividing line between public and private responsibilities. Foreign visitors, who are impressed by the accomplishments of American free enterprise, are often puzzled by the important role which the government plays in agriculture, housing, social security, or economic stabilization. Among Americans, there is lively controversy about the proper function of government, but it is rare to find disagreement among them on this basic principle: In a free enterprise system, the greatest possible degree of reliance must be placed on the individual, with the government taking action when and where needed in the interest of the general welfare.

In some countries, the "state" is conceived to be an entity apart from and superior to the people and the other institutions of the national society. It is thought of as a kind of higher being, having interests and goals of its own which take precedence over all others. The government, considered the visible earthly form of this transcendent state, is owed the obedience and wields the powers and privileges of the state. Such notions and attitudes are completely absent from American life. Americans think and talk only of "the government," not of "the state," and the former is in no sense endowed with the majesty credited in some countries to the latter. Here, the government is only one institution of society; furthermore, it is commonly regarded as the servant of the people. Its powers and privileges are limited by law and by custom, and its policies and activities to a much greater extent result from competing group interests than from the supposedly autonomous interests of the government itself.

Proposals for increases or decreases in the extent of government participation in the economic process usually require legislation, which means that they must survive not only the mutual checks and balances of the legislative and executive processes but often a subsequent review by the judiciary. Moreover, all citizens have the essential democratic right of advocating or opposing governmental policies and programs, and many specific interest groups have formed organizations designed to influence legislative or executive actions in behalf of their constituents. To reduce the possibility that they might misuse their economic power, the Congress has adopted laws regulating the activities of such "lobbying" organizations. Nonetheless, these and other constitutional and organizational arrangements are among the most important ways in which the American democracy ensures a reasonably satisfactory balance between governmental and private decision making in the democratic process.

Without exception, the written constitutions of the federal and state governments have been premised on the conviction that economic activity is a right of the individual, and that the government can regulate it in the public interest and can undertake economic activities of its own only in specified and limited ways. True, the government's powers and actions in the economic field have grown over the years, particularly in response to the unprecedented conditions of the twentieth century. But its role is still only a residual and supporting one, with decentralized private initiative continuing to occupy the center of the stage. Nor is there any disposition on the part of the American people today to make a fundamental change in this relationship.

There is no doubt that Americans still prefer to make their own decisions as managers, as farmers, as workers, and as consumers. They recognize, however, that a complex modern society cannot work without some regulations. To use a simile, motorists would resent it if someone told them when and where to drive their cars; but, with only a minimum of grumbling, they comply with the system of motor vehicle regulations without which there would be traffic chaos. There may be a great deal of discussion whether more or fewer traffic lights would expedite the flow of traffic, but there is no disagreement in principle that traffic lights are useful and compatible with the self-responsibility and self-reliance of the drivers.

Planning in the American Economy

A further source of confusion about the United States is the fact that there is much discussion here about planning even though the American economy is regarded as the opposite of a "planned economy." A planned economy is one in which the major decisions concerning production, investment, and consumption are made by a central authority. An economic plan for a period of years is laid down by the central authority, and the plan must be followed by the managers of production and distribution, who are functionaries of the state. Failure to live up to the plan makes these managers liable to severe punishment. This, indeed, is the very opposite of the American system.

The absence of an authoritative central plan does not mean, however, that there is no room for planning in the American economy. We have emphasized the significance of the fact that businessmen today make their investment decisions not merely in response to short-range market fluctuations but, increasingly, in recognition of long-run prospects. Business cannot pursue its objectives, such as the greatest amount of profits over a period of time, without an estimate of future markets for its products; future markets for one group of products can be appraised best in relation to the prospective growth of the economy as a whole. Similar considerations apply to economic decisions by farmers; and labor leaders could not engage in wage strategy; government could not appraise farm, water, and power development, social security, economic stabilization, or national defense programs, without planning each in relation to the potential growth and needs of the economy as a whole.

There may be differences of opinion among planners in business, labor unions, farm organizations, and government as to the exact pace of prospective economic growth, as to the effects of automation and other technological developments, as to the best rate of capital formation relative to consumption, and so on. These differences are subject to debate, and to some extent lead to general controversies which give substance to democratic processes. There is no difference of opinion, however, on the need for each decision maker—whether in business, labor, agriculture, or government—to *plan* his decisions.

Planning is not a monopoly of centrally regulated economies. It is an equally essential factor in a well-working free enterprise and free labor economy with democratic institutions. But the techniques of planning in centrally directed and in free economies are entirely different. A centrally directed economy requires a blueprint, which becomes a set of inflexible directives for the agents of production. In contrast, planning in a democracy requires each farmer or businessman or labor leader or government official to establish his own bench marks for the actions for which he is responsible. Furthermore, the better the economic planning by these private decision makers, the less the need for centralized planning.

Decentralized planning can be greatly aided if general "projections" of potential economic growth are made inside and outside the government. Such projections can serve as guides for the various decision makers, but it is the decision maker's own responsibility to select the projections which he prefers to use. The necessary degree of consistency among the private and public decisions is in part made possible by the fact that they are all using as a common frame of reference the prospective growth of the economy as a whole. This does not mean that there is or should be unanimity about the precisely desirable rate of economic growth; but rather that over time there has been slowly but surely developing a general acceptance of certain standards of economic performance which establish responsibilities and provide guides for action.

The various techniques of planning used in a free enterprise economy cannot be discussed here in detail.[1] We only want to emphasize that while the American economic system knows no central planning, it is an economy with a great deal of both private and public planning. Indeed, such planning is essential to the freedom and efficiency of the American system. One of the major purposes of the National Planning Association is to encourage and assist this kind of democratic planning by private groups and organizations and by government agencies.

The Depression of the 1930's and the Growth of the 1950's

A disquieting question may be lurking in the mind of the reader who has followed us to this point. He may be convinced that the

---

[1] For methods of democratic planning, see Gerhard Colm and Marilyn Young, *The American Economy in 1960,* National Planning Association, PP 81, Washington, D.C., December 1952, 166 pp.

American economic system functions well today. Why then did it not produce the same result during the depression of the 1930's? At that time, certain economists were busy explaining why, under the conditions of American society, economic stagnation had to be expected. In contrast, they recently have been explaining why continued prosperity is an almost innate characteristic of the American economy. What assurance is there that, overnight, America may not be back in a period of stagnation?

This crucial question should be raised; nothing could be so dangerous as to assume that the American economy has become immune to depressions. There are, however, decisive differences between the 1930's and the 1950's. In the 1930's, government action was haphazard, a mixture of reform and recovery measures, and met much skepticism and distrust—particularly in business circles. Now, we have certain checks and cushions which have been built into our economic structure, and which tend to mitigate possible downswings. The government—both the Executive Branch and the Congress—is organized to adopt anti-depression measures promptly when needed. Most important is a third factor: The major private groups and the public at large now expect and are prepared to support preventive action by the government. Agreement on this concept of the government's responsibility to take action in case of a downswing or inadequate growth could mean more ready acceptance of needed measures which might run counter to the more immediate or imagined interests of some groups. For these reasons there is a greatly increased confidence in the economic future which gives the private economy a much improved chance of continuing or resuming economic expansion.

Thus, unlike the 1930's, when fears of continued economic stagnation held sway, the 1950's are looked upon as the threshold of a new age of economic abundance. By mid-century, the United States had gone a long way toward eliminating the economic deficiencies of the "one-third of a nation" which President Roosevelt in his Second Inaugural Address called "ill-housed, ill-clad, ill-nourished." Today, the problems of poverty and economic distress are steadily being overcome. For those that persist, it is only a question of time before the future growth of the economy and the improvement of methods will almost certainly make possible their solution. If war can be avoided, the United States has the possibility of achieving material abundance for all within the next decade or two.

Assuming that America can meet the challenge of its potentialities, the average family could achieve by as early as 1965 a level of consumption 30 percent above today's standard, and the productive capacity of the country would permit a 40 percent increase in production. And Americans would also be able to meet more adequately the growing responsibilities for preserving and developing natural resources, providing needed community facilities, and improving education, health, and the care of the aged. But the elimination of poverty and of human suffering caused by economic deprivation would not mean that American society would have solved its major problems, or even all of its economic ones. Quite the contrary.

The Future Quality of Life

While America still confronts many serious and longstanding economic problems, it also faces new difficulties of a complex and baffling character which are being created, in part, by the very advances toward the elimination of poverty which we are making. These interrelated problems have to do with what might be called the quality of life in an age of quantitative material abundance.

We have reported in preceding chapters on American achievements and deficiencies in our efforts to improve living standards, maintain balanced economic growth, prevent excessive concentration of power, and mitigate other immediate, but relatively familiar, problems of the American economy. There is growing agreement on these objectives, and as desirable standards of economic behavior are further developed, the methods and techniques for dealing with these problems will improve. We have also discussed problems of more recent origin which only now are beginning to emerge clearly and to acquire urgency. These include particularly adapting our cities and metropolitan areas, our educational system, and other social institutions to the needs and consequences of population growth, the expansion of industry, the advancing conquest of poverty in the United States, and persisting international tensions.

Another group of questions, and one which will become increasingly important, is raised by the social, psychological, and moral problems which are likely to emerge in an age of material abundance. Among tasks to be met are the constructive use of increasing leisure time and the strengthening of individual creativity in the face of pressures for conformity and uniformity.

The continuing growth of productivity and intensified spread of automation will mean that Americans can produce vast quantities of goods and services with ever shorter hours of work and with less and less physical strain or drudgery. Judging from the recent past, there is ample evidence that Americans, given the necessary time and money, are prone to pursue vigorously whatever leisure-time activities may interest them personally. We have discussed some of the directions these activities have been taking, and there is no question that there has been a steady and encouraging increase in a wide variety of cultural, recreational, and handicraft activities. For the future, however, Americans may need to develop new forms of constructive activity in order to take full advantage of their growing opportunities for, and greater freedom in, choosing the ways they spend their nonworking hours. The challenge to American society, and particularly to the educational system, is so to develop the interests of Americans that their new-found leisure will find them willing and able to devote themselves to activities which are personally satisfying and are not socially harmful.

The increased danger of conformity and uniformity is the product of the complexity and interdependence of modern industrial economies, accompanied by the pressures created by the growth of population, the efforts to raise living standards, and continuing international tensions. Government agencies, business corporations, trade unions, and even universities and other private institutions have been compelled to increase their size, expand their functions, and rationalize their operations in order to cope effectively with the rigorous and changing conditions of the mid-twentieth century.

A major result of this trend is illustrated by the emergence of what William Whyte has called the "organization man," whose success depends upon convincing his superiors and his colleagues that he will not disturb the smooth working of the organization by advocating novel or unconventional ideas or by conducting himself in a noticeably individualistic manner. At the same time, the spread of middle-class and suburban standards of living to the large majority of Americans and pressures to conform to local social patterns also operate to reduce the scope of individuality and creativity. Hence, one of the main tasks in the age of approaching material abundance is the evolution of new ways by which people can find personal fulfillment in the life of the community without surrendering their individuality.

There are, however, characteristics of American society which counteract the tendencies toward greater conformity and uniformity. In the United States, almost everyone belongs to a variety of uncoordinated groups and organizations. The factory or office, the trade union, the church, the political party, the social club, and the neighborhood cultural and sports associations—each has its own claim on the loyalty of members and competes for their participation. In one sense, joining such organizations is itself an expression of conformity with current notions about the desirability of being active in community life. Nonetheless, a strong sense of belonging derived from meaningful participation in a particular church, party, trade union, or professional group frequently strengthens the individual's courage to resist less desirable and more general patterns of conformity. At the same time, such competing loyalities also help to ensure diversity of attitudes and interests, and thereby counteract pressures for excessive uniformity.

American concern about these tendencies can only be understood in the light of the traditional American ideal of individualism. The fate of individual creativity in American society will depend on the countervailing power of increasing awareness of the dangers; the open-minded and experimental attitude of most Americans; the growing sense of social responsibility on the part of business corporations, trade unions, and other large organizations; the universal conviction that government is the servant and not the master of the people; and many other institutions and values. So long as these characteristics of American society persist, there is hope that Americans will sooner or later find new and more effective ways of orchestrating individuality and community in the prospectively more difficult conditions of the coming decades.

Marxist Dogma and the American System

A large part of communism's strength is its unquestioned belief in the Marxist dogma. Many of the Marxist views have been subjected to revision, but one basic credo is essential for the devotion of its followers. This is that "capitalism" and the allegedly related "colonial imperialism" are doomed and that the communists, despite present difficulties, are riding the wave of the future. They are convinced that they are the vanguard of an army marching in accordance with an already determined world destiny.

The fact that the American system has made great advances in technological and managerial achievements is not denied by the communists. They frankly admit that they can learn, and want to learn, from American accomplishments in this respect. However, they are convinced that the more rapid these achievements in a free enterprise system, the nearer the day of its final collapse. They believe that only the communists can make lasting productive use of technological achievements regardless of where they have originated.

According to Marxism, capitalism is doomed by the necessity of so-called natural laws. The communists contend that this will happen in what seems to them the following logical way:

1. Technological advances make for the superiority of large over small firms.
2. The resulting concentration of capital goes hand in hand with a concentration of wealth and incomes in fewer and fewer hands. This leads to a gradual "proletarianization" of the middle classes and a growing gulf between the few wealthy and the many poor.

3. The inevitable existence of unemployment permits an exploitation of labor and makes for continued impoverishment of the masses.
4. The discrepancy between rising productive power and shrinking mass purchasing power and markets leads to the inescapable doom of capitalism, which can only temporarily be delayed by diverting production into armaments and international imperialistic ventures.

We believe that a survey of the American economy as it actually is refutes this Marxist argument step by step. The Marxist dogma was formulated in the light of the economic history of the nineteenth century and in answer to a laissez-faire interpretation of those developments. This dogma has no relevance if applied to the present American economy. However, being basic doctrine, it could not be abandoned by the communists.

Contrary to Marxist dogma, technological advances have made for the superiority of large enterprises in some branches of industry, but not in all. Nor has the degree of concentration in industrial capacity and capital gone hand in hand with a growing inequality in the distribution of income and wealth. The small and middle-sized enterprises have proved their superiority in many lines of activity. The middle classes have not been proletarianized; on the contrary, the status of what the Marxists love to call "the toiling masses" has been raised so high that they have largely merged into a growing middle class which includes most Americans. The economy of the American people has not resulted in impoverishment but has brought the people—all the people—of the United States to the threshold of abundance. Far from increasing the concentration of personal wealth and incomes in fewer and fewer hands, it has created a broadening of opportunities and more satisfactions for all.

Nor is mass unemployment an inevitable result of technological development. The theoretical insights and practical experiences of the past two decades suggest that a free enterprise society can, if it has the will to do so, prevent large-scale depressions and mass unemployment. The U. S. government is committed to such a policy of maintaining maximum employment, and this commitment is endorsed by both major political parties, by leaders of business, agriculture, and labor, and by the public generally. Continuing efforts are made to improve the techniques for carrying out this commitment.[2]

Large-scale armaments are a necessity forced upon the democracies by the exigencies of the world situation; they are a burden, and not an outlet for surplus production. There are a great many desirable tasks—domestic and international—which have had to be postponed

[2] See Gerhard Colm, editor, *The Employment Act, Past and Future, A Tenth Anniversary Symposium,* National Planning Association, SR 41, Washington, D.C., February 1956, 216 pp.

until a reduction in armaments becomes possible and releases productive resources for these constructive purposes.

Thus, American experience reveals the fallacies in the apparent logic of the Marxist doctrine. Our belief in the practical and moral worth of the American economic system is based both on this economic experience and on our conviction that what we have called the Jeffersonian concept of individual freedom and self-reliance is deeply ingrained in the human soul. We are convinced that the American system in the long run offers greater promise than any authoritarian system in productive and managerial efficiency; we know that it affords more freedom and self-responsibility than any totalitarian system.

What To Call the American Economic System

How are we to define this American economy, which confounds the observer who seeks to classify it in terms of traditional economic concepts?

The American system is capitalistic to the extent that the desire to make profit by privately owned and conducted activities is one of the major motivating factors of economic growth. It is a system of free enterprise, free labor, and free consumers. The American economy is not capitalistic, however, if capitalism means an arrangement in which the entrepreneur can do as he pleases and in which workers and consumers are exploited and the capitalist reaps the main benefits of economic activity. The American system is not capitalistic if capitalism means a government operating only in the interest of the entrepreneur. Nor is it capitalistic if capitalism is understood as nineteenth-century laissez-faire.

The American system is not socialistic if socialism is defined as an economy in which all or most factories are owned and operated by the state and the state determines what is to be produced, what new plants are to be built, what wages are to be paid, and so on. The American system is not socialistic if socialism means an arrangement in which the state plays the determining role in economic and social life.

In the American system, all institutions, public as well as private, are expected to serve the general well-being. In such a system, private enterprise is not an end in itself, but is the most effective form of organization for serving the needs of the people with a minimum of government regulation. In such a system also, the government is not an end in itself but is organized to fulfill the functions which cannot be adequately discharged by private enterprise.

Thus, the American system is neither capitalism nor socialism in the historical meanings of the terms. It cannot be classified under these headings because it is dominated neither by the state nor by private business nor by any other single group. All the institutions—public and private—play their roles with a great deal of self-determination and self-responsibility.

Who, then, is the master who, in the last analysis, provides the yardstick for judging what a responsible performance is? The answer to this crucial question is difficult to give and that is why it is difficult to define the American system precisely. We would probably come closest to the truth by saying that the American economic system serves the national interest of the American people—as expressed through democratic political processes, articulate public opinion, the multiplicity of private groups and organizations, and the attitudes of all Americans as individual consumers.

The "national interest," vague and fluid as the concept may be, has become more tangible than in the past. The advocates of laissez-faire frowned on any attempt to develop economic standards, such as desirable levels of consumption or housing or a desirable rate of economic expansion. If everybody only pursued his own self-interest, they contended, the best possible economic result would follow. Today there are emerging specific ideas about the desirable performance of an economy—jobs for those able and willing to work; avoidance of heavy fluctuations in employment, production, and prices; adequate wages, housing, nutrition, and health services; and a rate of economic growth which uses the advances of science and technology, makes possible the elimination of poverty at home, and supports cooperation in the solution of world problems. It is no longer taken for granted that the unrestrained pursuit of self-interest either by individuals or by organized groups will necessarily lead to the desired results. Individuals and organized groups are expected to pursue their self-interests in a way that will serve the requirements of the national interest.

Only a part of the requirements of the national interest have become crystalized into laws. Some are in the form either of "unwritten laws" and traditions or of the individual choices of men and women who are free to make both political and economic decisions. The general public accepts large enterprises, large unions, and large government as useful institutions, but does not want the political, economic, and social life of the people determined by any one of them. Those in charge of large enterprises or large unions or large government agencies are aware of this attitude and are learning more and more to respect it. Thus, for example, regardless of whether the antitrust laws cover all instances of possible abuse of economic power, the unwritten law does provide a punishment for actions by business corporations which violate the public interest. The punishment may consist of unfavorable publicity, with a possible adverse effect on sales of products or on the recruitment of needed personnel. It may consist of Congressional investigations, and of many other techniques for the expression of disapproval which exist in a democracy. Similarly, dissatisfaction either with inadequate governmental action or with over-extension of government power finds prompt expression in election returns.

This is a flexible structure. Very gradually, some of the unwritten laws crystallize and, after a process of democratic debate, become formalized into written laws. The laws, however, are not the most important aspects of this structure. In a way, they indicate only instances in which it has not worked well. Had there not been some misuse of economic power by private enterprise, there would have been no antitrust laws. Had there not been some substandard wages, there would have been no Wage-Hour Act. Had there been no severe depression, there probably would have been no Employment Act. The more responsive private groups are to the requirements of the general interest, the less the need for legislation and enforcement of standards by the government.

Thus, the economic system emerging in the United States embodies features of various "pure" economic systems, and promises to provide the capacity for reconciling the needs and values of the individual with the requirements of a complex society and the possibilities of modern technology.

A number of new names have been proffered by those who feel that a unique form of economic and social organization is developing on the American scene. The term "economic democracy" may well carry the connotation of responsiveness to the requirements of the general interest. However, economic democracy has also been understood to mean a very specific kind of workers' co-determination of management policies, which is not what we are talking about. "People's capitalism" has been suggested in the belief that the American economy is striving with capitalistic means for the well-being and dignity of all. This term correctly conveys the idea that the American system benefits not merely a few but virtually all the people. However, as we have seen, the American enterprise system has little similarity with what historically has been labeled as capitalism. Whatever the name chosen, it must accurately express the main characteristic of the American economy—its unique combination of individual freedom and social responsibility.

We by no means intend to suggest that the main characteristics of the American economy are peculiar only to the United States. Several of its significant features have originated in other countries in which free enterprise economies has undergone similar transformations. Only in this perspective, and at a loss for a better name, do we put forward *The Economy of the American People.*

The Economy of the American People—Is It for Export?

We have described the economy of the American people with considerable pride in its accomplishments and in the way it works out its own improvements. But what, if anything, can other countries learn from this American experience? Is the American system, in whole or in part, for export?

The American system has both universal and unique features. On the one hand, it expresses many of the fundamental values and aspirations that are common to all mankind, and it uses economic techniques which are used in many countries. On the other hand, the specific institutional embodiments of these values have been much influenced by the particular culture and traditions of the Western society within which they have evolved, and by the limitations and possibilities imposed by a particular geographical environment.

Insofar as other nations seek to achieve the same values of freedom, justice, and welfare as do Americans, they can adapt to their own situations many of the attitudes and techniques which have characterized American pursuit of these objectives. For example, the freedom and diversity of insight and initiative which result from the large measure of decentralized and private decision making in the United States are valued by many other countries. American attitudes toward work and workmanship; toward innovation and enterprise; toward mutual help and cooperation regardless of so-called class differences; toward practical experience, rather than traditional doctrine, as a guide to action—all these are suited to, and in varying degrees are characteristic of, other countries. Similarly, because of their efficiency, American productive techniques and managerial methods are spreading throughout the world under a wide variety of different forms of economic organization.

American experience has a profound significance for other countries particularly in two respects:

1. It shows that rapid economic growth—in contrast to largely futile attempts to redistribute a fixed national income—provides the necessary condition for increasing the economic welfare of all the people and achieving greater social justice in the society.
2. It shows that substantial economic growth can be accomplished without sacrificing individual freedom, initiative, and self-responsibility.

In effect, American society has been achieving an historically unique reconciliation of three partially conflicting human ideals—economic welfare, social justice, and individual freedom. Such a reconciliation can never be complete, but it has gone further in the United States than in most other societies and gives promise of progressing even further in the future. The fact that so substantial a reconciliation can actually be accomplished is certainly a message of great significance to all humanity. Other countries with different cultural and environmental limitations and possibilities may find some of the specific American institutional forms of private enterprise uncongenial to their traditions or irrelevant to their present conditions. In this brief report, we cannot specify the differences in economic organizations which may be warranted between, for example, a highly industrialized country in the Western cultural tradition and a predominantly agrarian country with an entirely different cultural background. Again, owing to rapidly growing populations and rising economic expectations, some densely populated but inadequately developed countries are in a situation in which they must strive to condense into a few decades the amount of economic development and expansion which the United States took over a century to achieve. In such circumstances, the governments of these countries are likely to assume more initiative in economic development than the U.S. government has undertaken.

Thus, it is important to distinguish between those features of the American system which are relevant to the needs and possibilities of other countries, and those which are not. Failure to make this distinction is largely responsible for the misunderstandings, both at home and abroad, over the "exportability" of the American economic system. There are some Americans who insist that other countries can make substantial economic progress only if they adopt the specific institutional forms of the American economy as well as its attitudes and techniques. There are Europeans and Asians who claim that nothing in the American experience has any relevance for their very different cultures and traditions. Both views are equally erroneous, for neither recognizes that probably the major contribution which the American people have been making in this century to the progress and welfare of mankind is the unique combination of attitudes and techniques they have evolved for achieving high productivity and living standards without sacrifice of freedom and individuality.

It is true that communist dictatorship also has achieved remarkably rapid economic expansion, high rates of capital formation, and fast technological advances in the Soviet Union. However, these have been purchased at the price not only of the suppression of political and individual freedom but also of forcing productive resources into armaments and industrialization with utter disregard for the welfare of the people. It is our conviction that balanced economic growth can be obtained without resort to terror, not only in advanced industrialized nations but in all countries of the world.

If there is any one theme which recurs in all kinds of variations throughout American history it is the need to reconcile the Hamiltonian idea of economic progress with the Jeffersonian ideal of individual self-reliance.

Economic progress has been achieved beyond all expectations. The increases in income and wealth, in factories and equipment, are there for everyone to see and to compare with the income and wealth of former times and other places. Whether in this process the Jeffersonian ideal of self-reliance has been lost or maintained cannot be determined by statistics. However, we have seen that strong movements have sprung up repeatedly to offset the feared preponderance of the large corporation in industry, transportation, and finance, and to protect agriculture and small business. These movements have left a deep impact on American legislation and possibly an even deeper, and in the end more effective, impact on what we have called "the general public" and on the present attitudes of business, labor, farmers, and the government. Jeffersonian ideals of self-responsibility and self-reliance are truly alive even in our industrial society.

Jefferson was mistaken in his belief that this spirit—which was for him the essence of America—could exist only on the family farm and in the artisan's small shop. True, a spirit of mutual respect could hardly develop in shops and factories during the period when the entrepreneur insisted on his absolute right as "master in his own house"—a period when industry usually involved sweated labor, economic insecurity, and poor housing, with all their bad consequences for family life. That period is now part of the past. Modern technology and modern working and living conditions are much more conducive to the existence of workers who are proud of their place in society and command the respect of all other groups.

But there is no assurance that the Jeffersonian spirit—vigorous as it is today—will automatically survive the future developments of the urban and industrial age. That it can live in managers and employees working in mutual respect and cooperation, is proved by present achievements. Indeed, this spirit is also alive in government officials, who are imbued with the conviction that their function is not to rule but to serve the common good of all the people. Thus, while there is no certainty, there is a good chance that vital democracy, which gives free play to self-reliant individuals, not only will survive, but will be intensified in the coming phase of industrial society.

The past and present achievements of American society reflect the rationalistic, pragmatic, and optimistic character of its people. Although these qualities hold great promise for America's future, they are capable of being misapplied. There can be, on the one hand, utopian expectations—the illusion that all individual and social problems can be readily solved by the application of human reason and the manipulations of "social engineering." There can be, on the other hand, complacency and self-satisfaction with what has already been done, which can blind Americans to the need for further changes and improvements. Adoption by Americans of either of these extreme attitudes could be fatal.

That both extremes can be avoided is evidenced by the growth during the last two decades of new and more profound conceptions of the nature and possibilities of man and society. These recognize that human reason, though powerful, is not omnipotent; that man's nature has limitless capacities not only for good but also for evil; and that social progress is possible even though perfection can never be grasped. In the courage to strive, despite the impossibility of complete or final victory, lies the best assurance both of the survival of individual freedom and of the increase in human welfare.

Appendix

Appendix Table 1

Economic Growth Indicators, 1929-1957

(Dollars in 1956 prices)

Year	Gross national product (billions)	Civilian employment (millions)	GNP per employed worker	Personal consumption expenditures (billions)	Population (millions)	Consumption expenditures per capita
1929	$186.8	47.6	$3,924	$128.9	121.9	$1,057
1930	169.2	45.5	3,719	121.5	123.2	986
1931	156.7	42.4	3,696	117.9	124.1	950
1932	133.4	38.9	3,429	107.2	124.9	858
1933	129.8	38.8	3,345	104.4	125.7	831
1934	143.5	40.9	3,509	110.1	126.5	870
1935	158.2	42.3	3,740	116.9	127.4	918
1936	179.1	44.4	4,034	128.9	128.2	1,005
1937	190.0	46.3	4,104	133.5	129.0	1,035
1938	181.2	44.2	4,100	131.5	130.0	1,012
1939	196.0	45.8	4,279	139.1	131.0	1,062
1940	213.3	47.5	4,491	146.4	132.1	1,108
1941	247.0	50.4	4,901	156.2	133.4	1,171
1942	278.3	53.8	5,173	153.4	134.9	1,137
1943	309.2	54.5	5,673	157.5	136.7	1,152
1944	332.1	54.0	6,150	163.0	138.4	1,178
1945	325.2	52.8	6,159	174.0	139.9	1,244
1946	290.1	55.3	5,246	194.2	141.4	1,373
1947	289.0	58.0	4,983	197.3	144.1	1,369
1948	302.4	59.4	5,091	201.2	146.6	1,372
1949	301.7	58.7	5,140	206.4	149.2	1,383
1950	329.8	60.0	5,497	218.7	151.7	1,442
1951	354.2	61.0	5,807	220.2	154.4	1,426
1952	366.9	61.3	5,985	227.2	157.0	1,447
1953	382.0	62.2	6,141	236.8	159.6	1,484
1954	375.6	61.2	6,137	241.2	162.4	1,485
1955	402.5	63.2	6,369	258.4	165.3	1,563
1956	414.7	65.0	6,380	267.2	168.2	1,589
1957	418.2	65.3	6,404	271.9	171.2	1,588

SOURCE: *Economic Indicators: 1957 Historical Supplement*, Joint Economic Committee, Washington D. C., 1957; U. S. Department of Commerce, Office of Business Economics; *Economic Report of the President*, January 1958.

Appendix Table 2

Index of Output per Man-hour for Selected Years, 1909-1956 (1909=100)

Year	Total	Farm	Nonfarm	Manufacturing industries
1909	100.0	100.0	100.0	100.0
1919	112.8	104.8	114.0	114.4
1929	140.3	114.8	142.0	197.7
1938	171.7	138.9	176.5	253.4
1947–49	209.6	184.5	205.8	282.5
1956	263.9	252.0	253.9	377.1

NOTE: Farm and nonfarm private production is divided by an estimate of man-hours employed in private production. Production is measured in constant dollars of the 1947 price level. For manufacturing industries, the Federal Reserve index of production has been used. The data have been shifted to a 1909 base-year index.

SOURCE: *Productivity, Prices, and Incomes*, Joint Economic Committee staff report, Washington, D. C., 1957, p. 89.

Appendix Table 3

Average Annual Rate of Increase in Output Per Man-hour for Selected Industries, 1947-1956[1]

(In percent per year)

MANUFACTURING	
Canning and preserving	5.1
Cement[2]	5.8
Clay construction products[2]	4.0
Paper and pulp	4.3
Primary smelting and refining (copper, lead and zinc)[2]	4.2
Rayon and synthetic fiber[2]	10.7
Steel	3.2
MINING	
Anthracite coal	4.9
Bituminous coal	5.6
Copper (recoverable metal)	2.5
Iron (usable ore)	1.2
SERVICES	
Railroad transportation (revenue traffic)	4.1
Telegraph[3]	−.9

[1] Refers to output in physical units per man-hour of work. Man-hour estimates are for production workers only.

[2] 1947–55.

[3] Output per employee.

SOURCES: *Indexes of Output per Man-hour for Selected Industries, 1929 to 1956*, U. S. Department of Labor, Bureau of Labor Statistics, Washington, D. C., BLS 558–0964.

Appendix Table 4

Disposable Income Received by Highest 5 Percent of Income Earners

(Percent of total)

1914	32.0
1920	24.0
1929	34.7
1939	26.8
1950	15.8
1952	15.8

SOURCE: Warren J. Bilkey, "Equality of Income Distribution and Consumption Expenditures," *The Review of Economics and Statistics*, February 1956, p. 84.

Appendix Table 5

Average Hourly Earnings for Selected Industries, 1939-1956

	Dollars per hour		Index of increase	
	1939	1956	1939	1956
Farm[1]	0.16	0.86	100	537
Textile mill products	0.46	1.45	100	315
Lumber and wood products	0.49	1.76	100	359
Furniture and fixtures	0.52	1.69	100	325
Retail trade	0.54	1.57	100	291
Paper and allied products	0.59	1.94	100	329
Chemicals and allied products	0.65	2.10	100	325
Machinery (except electrical)	0.75	2.21	100	295
Telephone	0.82	1.86	100	227
Bituminous coal mining	0.89	2.81	100	316
Automobiles	0.93	2.35	100	253
Consumer price index (1939=100)			100	196

[1] Average wage rate per hour without board or room; average daily wage rate divided by average hours worked per day.

SOURCES: W. S. Woytinsky, *Employment and Wages in the United States*, The Twentieth Century Fund, New York, 1953, p. 459; *Statistical Abstract of the United States, 1957*, U. S. Department of Commerce, Washington, D. C., 1957.

Appendix Table 6

Minutes of Working Time Required to Buy Various Foods

Commodity	United States (Sept. '51)	France (Paris) (Oct. '51)	Germany (Sept. '51)	Italy (Sept. '51)	U.S.S.R. (Moscow) (Apr. '52)
Flour, wheat (lb.)	4	20	15	15	27
Bread (lb.)	6	9	12	13	14
Beef (lb.)	31	126	n.a.	128	132
Fish (lb.)	18	33	31	65	135
Butter (lb.)	30	135	115	162	270

(Continued)

Appendix Table 6– (Continued)

Minutes of Working Time Required to Buy Various Foods

Commodity	United States (Sept. '51)	France (Paris) (Oct. '51)	Germany (Sept. '51)	Italy (Sept. '51)	U.S.S.R. (Moscow) (Apr. '52)
Cheese (lb.)	22	104	n.a.	109	n.a.
Milk (qt.)	8	16	15	20	42
Eggs (doz.)	32	118	125	126	187
Apples (lb.)	4	19	16	n.a.	89
Potatoes (lb.)	2	3	3	5	9
Oleomargarine (lb.)	13	64	39	n.a.	152
Sugar (lb.)	21	21	21	37	110

n.a. Not available.

NOTE: It should be emphasized that differences in the importance of the various food items in the consumption pattern of the population limit the extent to which such comparisons can be conclusive as a measure of living standards.

SOURCE: "Food-Purchasing Power of Earnings in 12 Countries 1951–52," *Monthly Labor Review*, June 1952.

Appendix Table 7

Nativity and Parentage of the White Population of the United States, 1870-1950

Year	Total white population	Total foreign white stock	Foreign born	Native-born of foreign or mixed parentage
	(In thousands)			
1870	33,589	10,818	5,494	5,324
1880	43,403	14,835	6,560	8,275
1890	55,101	20,626	9,122	11,504
1900	66,809	25,860	10,214	15,646
1910	81,732	32,243	13,346	18,898
1920	94,821	36,399	13,713	22,686
1930	110,287	39,886	13,983	25,902
1940	118,702	34,577	11,419	23,158
1950	134,942	33,751	10,161	23,589
	(In percent of total white population)			
1870	100.0	32.2	16.4	15.9
1880	100.0	34.2	15.1	19.1
1890	100.0	37.4	16.6	20.9
1900	100.0	38.7	15.3	23.4
1910	100.0	39.5	16.3	23.1
1920	100.0	38.4	14.5	23.9
1930	100.0	36.2	12.7	23.5
1940	100.0	29.1	9.6	19.5
1950	100.0	25.0	7.5	17.5

SOURCES: *Historical Statistics of the United States, 1789–1945*, U. S. Department of Commerce, Washington, D. C., 1945; *Statistical Abstract, 1957, op. cit.*

Appendix Table 8

Status of Education

Country	Illiteracy rate[1]	Students enrolled, 1954: Number[2] (millions)	Students enrolled, 1954: Percent of total population
United States	2 (1952)	36.1	22
Belgium	3 (1947)	1.6	18
Greece	24 (1951)	1.2	15
Philippines	38 (1948)	4.1	19
Portugal	42 (1950)	.9	10
Ecuador	44 (1950)	.4	11
Thailand	46 (1947)	3.2	16
Brazil	51 (1950)	5.5	10
Turkey	65 (1950)	1.9	8
Egypt	75 (1947)	2.0	9
India	82 (1951)	27.7	7
Haiti	89 (1950)	.3	9

[1] Number of persons aged ten and over who cannot read and write as a percent of the total population aged ten and over. For the United States, data apply only to illiterates in population fourteen years and over.

[2] Number of students enrolled includes pre-school, primary, secondary, technical, teacher-training, and high (post-secondary) classes. For Portugal, India, Ecuador, and United Kingdom—1953; for Turkey—1952.

SOURCES: *United Nations Statistical Yearbook, 1956; Monthly Bulletin of Statistics*, United Nations, April 1957; *Statistical Abstract, 1957, op. cit.*

Appendix Table 9

Days Lost Through Work Stoppages per Employee[1]

(Annual average, 1950-1954)

Country	Days	Country	Days
United States	1.4	Canada	.7
Finland	1.8	Belgium	.6
New Zealand	1.2	Germany, Federal Republic	.1
Australia	.9	Norway	.1
India	.9	Sweden	.1
Italy	.9	United Kingdom	.1
France	.8	Denmark	[2]
Ireland	.8	Netherlands	[2]
Japan	.8	South Africa	[2]

[1] Data refer to mining, manufacturing, construction, and transportation industries only.

[2] Less than .05 days per employee.

SOURCE: "Industrial Disputes 1937–54," *International Labour Review*, July 1955.

Appendix Table 10

Average Annual Rate of Return Before Taxes, U. S. Manufacturing Corporations by Asset Size (Profits as a percent of stockholder's equity)

Year	Corporate assets under $250,000	Corporate assets $1,000 million and over
1956	19.9	22.7
1955	10.7	26.8
1954	7.8	21.3
1953	12.4	25.1
1952	17.0	23.6
1951	17.2	29.4
1950	16.8	29.4
1949	9.8	23.2
1948	15.5	26.1

SOURCE: *Quarterly Financial Report for Manufacturing Corporations* (for the years 1948–56), Federal Trade Commission and Securities and Exchange Commission, Washington, D. C.

Appendix Table 11

Growth of Science and Technology

Year	Labor force (thousands)	Scientists and Engineers	
		Number (thousands)	Percent of labor force
1930	48,600	261	.5
1940	52,900	378	.7
1950	60,000	740	1.2
1956	68,800	950	1.4

SOURCE: *Trends in Employment and Training of Scientists and Engineers*, National Science Foundation, Washington, D. C., 1956.

Appendix Table 12

Private Foreign Investments in the United States, 1914 (In millions of dollars)

Source	Type of Investment			
	Rails	Other American securities	Foreign controlled enterprises	Total
Great Britain	2,800	850	600	4,250
Germany	300	350	300	950
Netherlands	300	200	135	635
France	290	75	45	410
Canada	130	95	50	275
All others	350	140	80	570
Total	4,170	1,710	1,210	7,090

SOURCE: Cleona Lewis, *America's Stake in International Investments*, Brookings Institution, Washington, D. C., 1938.

Appendix Table 13

The Nation's Economic Budget, 1929 and 1956
(In billions of current dollars)

Economic group	1929 Receipts	1929 Expenditures	1929 Excess of Receipts	1956 Receipts	1956 Expenditures	1956 Excess of Receipts
Consumers						
Disposable personal income	83.1			287.2		
Personal consumption expenditures		79.0			267.2	
Personal savings (+)			+4.1			+20.0
Business						
Gross retained earnings	11.5			40.9		
Gross private domestic investment		16.2			65.9	
Excess of investment (−)			−4.7			−25.0
International						
Net foreign investment		.7			1.4	
Excess of investment (−)			−.7			−1.4
Government (federal, state, and local)						
Tax and nontax receipts or accruals	11.2			109.0		
Less: Transfers, interest, and subsidies	1.7			24.0		
Equals: net receipts	9.5			85.0		
Total government expenditures		10.2			104.2	
Less: transfers, interest, and subsidies		1.7			24.0	
Equals: purchases of goods and services		8.5			80.2	
Surplus (+)			+1.0			+4.8
Statistical discrepancy	+.3		+.3	+1.6		+1.6
Gross national product	104.4	104.4	—	414.7	414.7	—

Source: *1954 National Income Supplement to the Survey of Current Business;* and *Survey of Current Business, op. cit.,* July 1957.

Appendix Table 14

The Nation's Spending for Major Categories, 1956
(In billions of dollars)

1. Basic consumer needs		
a) Food	71.3	
b) Clothing	25.3	
c) Shelter	32.8	
d) Household operation	13.3	
Total		142.7

(Continued)

2. Other consumer requirements		
a) Household furnishings	22.8	
b) Personal business services	14.0	
c) Personal care	3.6	
Total		40.4
3. Transportation		
a) Purchases of new and used cars	12.0	
b) Expenditures for upkeep and operation	15.0	
c) Purchased local and intercity transportation	3.3	
Total		30.3
4. Consumer luxuries and semi-luxuries		
a) Smoking and drinking	15.0	
b) Communication	5.6	
c) Toys and sports equipment	3.0	
d) Spectator amusements	1.8	
e) Other recreational activities	3.4	
f) Foreign travel and personal remittances abroad	2.4	
g) Jewelry and watches	1.7	
Total		32.9
5. Education		
a) Private expenditures	4.1	
b) Public expenditures	14.2	
Total		18.3
6. Research and development		
a) National security	2.2	
b) Other government research	.3	
c) Private research	4.5	
Total		7.0
7. Medical and hospital care		
a) Private expenditures	13.7	
b) Public expenditures	3.7	
Total		17.4
8. Private religious and welfare activities		4.5
9. Private capital investment		
a) Producers' durable equipment	28.1	
b) Residential construction	16.0	
c) Nonresidential building	15.6	
d) Net change in business inventories	4.6	
Total		64.3
10. National security expenditures (excluding research)		42.4
11. Other government activities		
a) Highways	7.0	
b) Sewer and water	1.3	
c) Other public services	11.6	
Total		19.9
12. Net foreign investment		1.4
Total national product		421.7

(Continued)

NOTES:

Total spending by major categories exceeds gross national product because research and development are here considered as capital investment items rather than as intermediate or current account items. Details may not add to totals due to rounding.

1-a) Excludes tobacco and alcoholic beverages.
b) Excludes jewelry and watches.
c) Includes current rental payments on existing houses, including imputed rent for owner-occupied houses.
d) Includes household utilities and telephone.

2-a) Includes furniture, appliances, other house furnishings, and domestic services.
b) Includes payments for financial, legal, insurance, and other services and for interest on personal debt, etc.
c) Includes barber shops, beauty parlors, toilet articles, etc.

3-b) Includes gasoline and oil, parts and accessories, repair, etc.

4-b) Includes books, magazines, newspapers, radio, television, phonograph, etc.
d) Includes motion pictures, operas, legitimate theatres, spectator sports.
e) Includes clubs, flowers and potted plants, pari-mutuel spending, etc.

5-a) and b) Includes expenditures for construction and operation.

6-a) and b) Estimated on the basis of Budget data.

7-a) and b) Includes expenditures for construction, medicine, professional services, and burial expenses.

8. Includes construction.

9-c) Excludes educational, hospital, and religious institutions.

SOURCES: *Summary of Governmental Finances in 1956,* Bureau of the Census, Series G-GF56, August 23, 1957; *Survey of Current Business,* July 1957; 1958 Budget of the United States.

Appendix Table 15

Economic Growth Potential, 1956-1965

	Actual 1956	Projected 1965
Population (millions)	168.2	190.3
Civilian labor force	67.5	76.2
Unemployed (millions)	2.6	3.0
Employed (millions)	64.9	73.2
Agriculture (millions)	6.6	5.5
Nonagriculture (millions)	52.3	60.2
Government (millions)	6.0	7.5
Average weekly hours (number)		
Agriculture (number)	44.9	44.0
Nonagriculture (number)	38.8	37.5
Total average (number)	39.5	38.0
Private output per man-hour (1956 $)	$ 3.13	4.10
Agriculture (1956 $)	1.30	1.85
Nonagriculture (1956 $)	3.40	4.35
Government product per employee (1956 $)	$6,000	$7,500

(Continued)

Appendix Table 15 (Continued)

Economic Growth Potential, 1956-1965

	Actual 1956	Projected 1965
Gross national product (billions 1956 $)		
Agriculture (billions 1956 $)	$ 20.0	$ 23.5
Nonagriculture (billions 1956 $)	358.6	508.0
Government (billions 1956 $)	36.1	52.5
Total (billions 1956 $)	$414.7	$584.0

SOURCES: 1956—*Economic Indicators: 1957 Historical Supplement; Survey of Current Business*, July 1957; 1965—National Planning Association.

Appendix Table 16

Gross National Product

Calendar Year 1956 and Alternative Projections for 1965 (Billions of dollars in 1956 purchasing power)

	1956	1965 I	1965 II	1965 III
Gross national product	414.7	584.0	584.0	600.0
National security expenditures	42.4	46.5	20.0	66.5
Personal consumption expenditures	267.2	385.0	395.0	377.5
Private domestic investment	65.9	88.0	91.0	95.0
Net foreign investment	1.4	1.5	4.0	1.0
Government purchases, other than for national security	37.8	63.0	74.0	60.0

SOURCES: *Economic Indicators: 1957 Historical Supplement;* 1965—National Planning Association.

NOTE:

For illustrative purposes three alternative full employment models of the gross national product are presented: one assumes no disarmament; one assumes a cut in national security programs to about one-half the present level; the third considers the possibility that security expenditures will be increased. The calendar year 1965 will serve as the bench mark for the projection, assuming that any major change in armament programs will take place in stages during the period between 1960 and 1965. 1956 serves as the base year and all estimates are expressed in 1956 prices. The GNP projection for 1965 is based on the principal determinants as set forth in Appendix Table 15. In the event that a substantial increase in defense expenditures becomes necessary, it is assumed that the growth of the national product will be accelerated as a result of additional people entering the labor force, working longer hours, etc.

Alternative I assumes continuation of current programs for national security with an increase in nondefense government programs approximately in line with the rise in total production. Alternative II assumes that a $26-27 billion reduction in national security programs is compensated by an increase in personal consumption, in domestic and foreign investments, and in nondefense government programs. Alternative III assumes that we will have to increase our national security programs by $20 billion.

Appendix Table 17

Possible Increases in Nondefense Expenditure Programs, 1956-1965

	(billion)
Highways, skyways, metropolitan access roads, and other means of transportation	$ 8.0
School construction	4.0
Education, operating expenses	11.0
Urban water supply and water conservation	3.0
Hospitals	2.5
Miscellaneous public works	2.5
Other government activities (excluding social security benefits and interest payments)	5.0
Total	$36.0

SOURCE: See Appendix Table 16; also Statement of Gerhard Colm before the Subcommittee on Dis armament of the Senate Foreign Relations Committee, March 7, 1957.

NOTE:

Estimates for those areas in which future additions to government expenditures may be most appropriate in the event of a substantial reduction in armaments are offered only as a very rough indication of possible increases in nondefense programs, particularly of state and local governments. Alternative II for 1965 (see Appendix Table 16) assumes a $36 billion increase in our nondefense programs over those of the base year 1956. This increase could be broken down in several ways among a number of different programs.

Appendix Table 18

Concentration Ratio of Selected Manufacturing Industries (Percent accounted for by each industry's four largest companies)

Manufacturing industry	Value of Shipments 1947	Value of Shipments 1954	Employment 1950	Employment 1954
High-concentration industries:				
Primary aluminum	100	100	100	100
Gypsum products	85	90	89	86
Telephone and telegraph equipment	96	89	90	88
Aluminum rolling and drawing	94	88	89	84
Steam engines and turbines	88	87	87	86
Soap and glycerin	79	85	69	71
Cigarettes	90	82	81	75
Synthetic fibers	78	80	76	73
Tin cans and other tinware	78	80	77	78
Tires and inner tubes	77	79	78	80
Transformers	73	78	77	71
Motor vehicles and parts	56	75	59	72
Computing and related machines	69	74	70	72
Tractors	67	73	76	72
Domestic laundry equipment	40	68	53[1]	60
Cane sugar refining	70	67	69	69

(Continued)

Appendix Table 18–(Continued)

Concentration Ratio of Selected Manufacturing Industries

(Percent accounted for by each industry's four largest companies)

Manufacturing industry	Value of Shipments 1947	Value of Shipments 1954	Employment 1950	Employment 1954
Blast furnaces	67	65	57[1]	63
Electronic tubes	73	64	64	63
Photographic equipment	61	63	61	61
Aircraft engines	72	62	55	51
Byproduct coke ovens	53	58	n.a.	53
Steel works and rolling mills	45	54	55	53
Copper rolling and drawing	60	53	51	54
Motors and generators	59	50	57	47
Low-concentration industries:				
Confectionery products	17	19	12	15
Paper and paperboard	n.a.	19	14	18
Construction and mining machinery	18	19	16	19
Machine tools	20	19	25	20
Cotton broad-woven fabrics	n.a.	18	15	18
Newspapers	21	18	16	14
Leather tanning and finishing	27	18	18	17
Structural and ornamental work	23	18	20	16
Poultry dressing plants	32	17	33[1]	19
Valves and fittings	24	17	21	22
Paperboard boxes	18	16	12	13
Metal stampings	17	14	n.a.	12
Men's suits and coats	9	11	13	11
Commercial printing	9	10	9	10
Wood furniture	7	8	6	7
Machine shops	n.a.	8	12	8
Plastic products	n.a.	8	n.a.	7
Sawmills and planing mills	5	7	4	5
Women's suits and coats	n.a.	3	n.a.	4

n.a. Comparable data not available.

[1] 1935.

SOURCE: *Concentration in American Industry*, Report of Subcommittee on Antitrust and Monopoly, 85th Congress, 1st Session, Washington, D. C., 1957, Tables 44 and 58.

NOTE:

Industries of high concentration are those in which the four largest corporations in an industry account for more than 50 percent of the total shipping in that industry. Industries of medium concentration are those in which this ratio is between 20 and 50 percent; industries of low concentration are those in which the ratio is less than 20 percent.

It should be noted, however, that other measures of concentration ratios (sales, income, assets, etc.) and other criteria for industry concentration have been used to indicate trends in monopoly power. For example, the magnitude of these ratios of concentration depends in part upon the definition of the particular industry or activity to be measured. The 75 percent concentration ratio for shipments for the motor vehicles and parts industry would be 98 percent if applied to shipments of passenger cars alone.

NPA OFFICERS AND BOARD OF TRUSTEES

NPA PUBLICATIONS POLICY

NPA is an independent, nonpolitical, nonprofit organization established in 1934. It is an organization where leaders of agriculture, business, labor, and the professions join in programs to maintain and strengthen private initiative and enterprise.

Those who participate in the activities of NPA believe that the tendency to break up into pressure groups is one of the gravest disintegrating forces in our national life. America's number-one problem is that of getting diverse groups to work together for this objective: To combine our efforts to the end that the American people may always have the highest possible cultural and material standard of living without sacrificing our freedom. Only through joint democratic efforts can programs be devised which support and sustain each other in the national interest.

NPA's Standing Committees—the Agriculture, Business, and Labor Committees on National Policy and the Committee on International Policy—and its Special Committees are assisted by a permanent research staff. Whatever their particular interests, members have in common a fact-finding and socially responsible attitude.

NPA believes that through effective private planning we can avoid a "planned economy." The results of NPA's work will not be a grand solution to all our ills. But the findings, and the process of work itself, will provide concrete programs for action on specific problems, planned in the best traditions of a functioning democracy.

NPA's publications—whether signed by its Board, its Committees, its staff, or by individuals—are issued in an effort to pool different knowledges and skills, to narrow areas of controversy, and to broaden areas of agreement.

All reports published by NPA have been examined and authorized for publication under policies laid down by the Board of Trustees. Such action does not imply agreement by NPA Board or Committee members with all that is contained therein, unless such endorsement is specifically stated.

NATIONAL PLANNING ASSOCIATION

A Voluntary Association Incorporated under the Laws of the District of Columbia

1606 NEW HAMPSHIRE AVE., N. W., WASHINGTON 9, D. C.

JOHN MILLER: *Assistant Chairman* and *Executive Secretary*

EUGENE H. BLAND: *Editor of Publications*

7